WRITERS THREE: A LITERARY EXCHANGE

Claude Houghton, c.1948

WRITERS THREE: A LITERARY EXCHANGE

On the Works of Claude Houghton

with

Henry Miller
Claude Houghton
Ben Abramson

Introduction by
Ronald Gottesman

Roger Jackson, *Publisher*
Ann Arbor, Michigan

❄1995❄

ISBN (trade) = 0-9634136-1-5
ISBN (signed) = 0-96342356-1-7

For information contact the publisher:

Roger Jackson
339 Brookside Drive
Ann Arbor, Michigan 48105

SPECIAL THANKS TO:

Miss Gilda (Kaye) Cantouris for permission to publish the Claude Houghton letters and essays; to Valentine Miller, Tony Miller and Barbara Miller Sandford for permission to publish the Henry Miller letters and essays; and to Deborah Benson for permission to publish the letters and essays of Ben Abramson.

And a sincere note of appreciation to John W. Bagnole and Anthony Chamberlaine-Brothers, who freely spent hours of their time proofing and commenting on this manuscript; to Ronald Gottesman who wrote the introduction at a time when he had numerous other projects waiting for his attention; to William E. Ashley for his review and comments; and to Andrew Makowsky for his enthusiasm for this project as well as his assistance in supplying many of the quotes which appear in the "Critical Reviews" section of this work.

ACKNOWLEDGEMENTS

"Discovering Claude Houghton" is an excerpt from *The Books in My Life*, Copyright © 1969 by New Directions Publishing Corporation.

"Henry Miller's Apocalyptic Aspect" was first published under the title "British Notes" when it appeared in *The Happy Rock: A Book About Henry Miller*, edited and published by Bern Porter, 1945. It has recently reappeared under the current title in *Henry Miller: A Book of Tributes, 1931-1994*, Copyright © 1994 by Craig Peter Standish.

"Claude Houghton and the Novel of the Future" by Ben Abramson first appeared in *Reading and Collecting*, Volume 2 No. 1, December 1937.

"Preface to *I am Jonathan Scrivener*" by Henry Miller originally appeared in the French edition of *Je suis Jonathan Scrivener*, published by Corrêa, in 1954.

"Original Preface to the Miller-Houghton Letter of January 31, 1942" first appeared in Catalogue 30 of the Argus Book Shop, spring 1948.

PHOTOGRAPH CREDITS

Frontispiece photograph of Claude Houghton supplied through the courtesy of Anthony Chamberlaine-Brothers; Ben Abramson's photograph which appears on the dedication page was made available by Deborah Benson; the photograph of Henry Miller which appears on page eight was provided by Sam Griffith.

Alphabetical listing of the major works of Claude Houghton that are discussed in this literary exchange:

All Change, Humanity!
Chaos is Come Again
Christina
Hudson Rejoins the Herd
I am Jonathan Scrivener
Julian Grant Loses His Way
Kingdoms of the Spirit
Strangers
This was Ivor Trent

PUBLISHER'S NOTE:

Because the books of Claude Houghton are long out-of-print and nearly impossible to find, critical comments and brief summaries of many of the above titles are presented in this book, beginning on page 149. In addition, *Hudson Rejoins the Herd*, the Houghton book most discussed by Henry Miller and Ben Abramson, is extensively quoted in the "Notes, References..." section which begins on page 105.

Dedicated to the memory of Ben Abramson (1898-1955), who was the first to recognize the importance of Miller's letters to Claude Houghton, and to his daughter, Deborah Benson, who provided encouragement and generous cooperation in making this publication a reality.

Henry Miller, c. 1941

CONTENTS

Preface

—Roger Jackson

This book is the result of an accidental beginning and the answering of three circuitous questions. The accidental beginning occurred in March, 1989, while dining with my good friend Andrew Makowsky in an oriental restaurant on the Lower East Side in New York City. During that evening he asked me a question that I now know Ben Abramson had asked Henry Miller 48 years previously, almost to the day: "Have you ever read Claude Houghton?" I had not, but Andrew's expansive enthusiasm for this writer was very much apparent, and it was not a complete surprise when a couple weeks later a gift copy of Houghton's *I am Jonathan Scrivener* arrived in the mail.

A year and a half later, while perusing the Henry Miller-Ben Abramson correspondence at UCLA, I saw a double page proof of Ben Abramson's planned production of Miller's *Open Letter to Claude Houghton.* Also included in the correspondence file was Ben's "Preface," written in high spirited praise, such that a convincing argument was made that publication of Miller's letter to Houghton dated January 31, 1942, was literary history in the making. At the very least I thought it was worthy of publication (Ben's publication of it would never materialize) and I made plans to bring out in chapbook form not only the single letter Abramson had planned, but also three additional Miller-Houghton letters of that same year, all dealing with Houghton's works.

The circuitous questions followed naturally from my first reading of Abramson's "Preface." What specifically did Houghton write that created such a positive response in Miller? What did Miller write (in response to Houghton) that caused such an effect on Abramson? And finally, what did Abramson write (in response to Miller's response to Houghton) that piqued my interest so much, now that Andrew Makowsky had planted the seed? Being able to provide answers to these three questions, I expanded the scope of the Miller-Houghton book to include the correspondence of all three writers, their supporting essays, and healthy excerpts from Houghton's *Hudson Rejoins the Herd* so the reader can experience, first hand, this literary exchange and progression.

June 23, 1995
Ann Arbor, Michigan

Introduction: "The Imperfect Is Our Paradise"

—Ronald Gottesman

When I see the blindness and the wretchedness of man, when I regard the whole silent universe and man without light, left to himself and, as it were, lost in this corner of the universe, without knowing who has put him there, what he has come to do, what will become of him at death, and incapable of all knowledge, I become terrified, like a man who should be carried in his sleep to a dreadful desert island and should awake without knowing where he is and without means of escape. And thereupon I wonder how people in a condition so wretched do not fall into despair.

—Pascal

There is always chaos, and we must endure, as man has always endured.

—Ben Abramson

And, after all Ben, what the hell does it matter what happens to us so long as the vision of one's heart is a reality.

—Claude Houghton

The withdrawal from the world is not physical but spiritual. Then, too, it's only when we realize how utterly alone we are that we discover our kinships—and not merely with a chosen few, but with all humanity.

—Henry Miller

In *Writers Three: A Literary Exchange*, Roger Jackson has painstakingly assembled and annotated a fascinating compilation by and about three men whose minds and imaginations intersected during the Second World War. As Jackson's preface makes clear, the correspondences, criticism and excerpts he has brought together reveal two writers, Claude Houghton and Henry Miller, whose shared passion for social reality and metaphysical speculation was recognized immediately by bookseller Ben Abramson, even though he was more skeptical by temperament than either Houghton or Miller. Jackson has detailed their relationships carefully, and I won't repeat here what is elsewhere available in the volume. Rather, I will try to sketch a cultural context that may make certain central features of this compilation easier to understand for those not familiar with what historian Eric Hobsbawm has identified as the Age of Catastrophe.

In his *The Age of Extremes: A History of the World, 1914-1991* (1994), Hobsbawm reviews the escalating succession of increasingly brutal wars, ruthlessly repressive revolutions, long periods of world-wide economic crisis, the uncontrolled growth of fanaticisms both religious and secular, the spread of torture and genocide as acceptable instruments for resolution of "civil" conflicts, the loss of faith in political authority at all levels, that have brought us to anticipate, as Hobsbawm concludes, that the world will end with a bang *and* a whimper.

Of course, the sense of imminent disaster, of moral and spiritual collapse that Hobsbawm traces has a long history though it began to emerge powerfully toward the end of the 19th century, and, with some anomalous periods of optimism, has accelerated since then. In 1899, for example, Stephen Crane spoke of a universe in which human beings are so many lice clinging "to a whirling, fire-smote, ice-locked, disease-ridden, space-lost bulb." By the time Henry Miller first traveled to Europe in the late 1920s, T.S. Eliot had already announced in *The Wasteland*, "This is the dead land / This is cactus land" and noted "I should be glad of another death." His friend Ezra Pound, another American expatriate (like Eliot, more nearly exile than expatriate), had written the following memorable lines about the First World War in "Hugh Selwyn Mauberly":

> There died a myriad,
> And of the best, among them,
> For an old bitch gone in the teeth,
> For a botched civilization.

This summary judgement, of course, was shared by many English writers and intellectuals of whom George Orwell may be cited as one who shared Pound's assessment of war and economic inequities without losing his balance and looking to totalitarians of the left or right for utopian solutions.

Michael Fraenkel, a much less well-known thinker and writer than Eliot, Pound or Orwell, had befriended Miller while he was getting ready to write *Tropic of Cancer*, wrote eloquently of the temper of the times in which Abramson, Houghton and Miller came of age. The apprehension, fear and uncertainty of the 1920s, he wrote, "was like a mist, a fog, a condition of the weather, the air was thick with it." It was all-pervasive; it "settled over people's lives and homes, over their thoughts and feelings, words and acts; over everything they touched or handled, the clothing they wore, the food they ate, the books they read, the pictures they saw." Unlike Eliot or Pound, who found, respectively, traditional religious faith and radical utopian fascism as ways of dealing with the corrupt and corrupting conditions of the time, Fraenkel's antidote, like Miller's, was to accept the decay and corruption—"The Death," he called it—and use it homeopathically "*To come alive to himself.*"

By the time Abramson introduced Miller to Houghton's works, Miller had in fact concluded that the world had gone to hell and that he was glad of it since it meant the possibility, in a thousand years or so, of a new and better prospect for sane living. In his book on Rimbaud, *The Time of the Assassins*, Miller asserted: "let society scotch its own rotten corpse! Let us have a new heaven and a new earth!" He also rejoiced because these rejections absolved him from attempting to save or improve society and allowed him, without guilt, to pursue his own salvation—the salvation of joy of the moment, of pursuing his own identity while singing and dancing over the corpse of a depleted civilization devoted only to getting and spending, to cruelty and competition, to the mad pursuit of technology and materialism. As Miller put his credo in a letter written to Huntington Cairns on April 30, 1939, "The only relationship I acknowledge is with God." Among the most approving observations Miller made about Houghton is "You are an awakener," which recalls Thoreau's epigraph to *Walden*: "I do not propose to write an ode to dejection, but to brag as lustily as chanticleer in the morning, standing on his roost, if only to wake my neighbors up." Indeed, Miller saw himself as a legatee of the American Transcendentalists—Emerson, Thoreau, and Whitman in particular, and was especially sensitive to the vatic and prophetic strains he sensed in Houghton's writings.

Abramson initially recommended Houghton to Miller on the ground that "what man is and what man may become is his sole theme," and cited approvingly the critical view that Houghton's novels presented "the finest and most firmly thought-out exposition of the spiritual problem of modern times"—man's "utter loneliness of ...soul." In turn, Abramson could recommend Miller to Houghton as a "spiritual paratrooper"—a characterization, given Miller's detestation for war, that must have struck him as oxymoronic. (My guess is that Miller would have been amused by the way the metaphors of war had infected even his pacifist friend's imagination.)

For his part, Abramson, more commonsensical bookseller and publisher than artist, objected to the ending of one of Houghton's novels with the observation: "I do not believe that a gun can ever solve a human problem." What's all the shooting for? It sounds like Chicago." Moving from analysis of Houghton's novel to conditions in America, Abramson notes: "Here there has been little change. The news we get comes from official sources, and cannot be relied upon." Like Houghton and Miller, Abramson was in revolt against authority and profoundly suspicious of its representatives.

In spite of their skepticism, sense of doom, and even despair over the pain and evil all around them, however, all three of these men managed to imagine ideal societies, ideal writers, ideal books, ideal friends, ideal "unknowns," and ideal selves. This capacity for buoyancy in a time of lead is the implicit sub-text in all of their exchanges. "The world," Miller announced at the beginning of his career, "is a cancer eating itself away..." but, like Abramson and Houghton, he remained "Always merry and bright." Abramson was a realistic romantic, Houghton a mystical romantic, and Miller an incurable romantic. All three may have written off the corrupt world into which they had been born, but temperamentally they all maintained membership in the Party of Hope.

July 3, 1995
Santa Monica, California

Historical Note

—Roger Jackson

Henry Miller, Claude Houghton and Ben Abramson were contemporaries, varying in age by only eight years. Geographically, there was considerable distance between them—Houghton in England, Abramson in Chicago, and Miller in Paris, New York and California. What brought them together was a genuine interest in books, authors, and the process of writing.

Ben Abramson was born in Lithuania in 1898 and immigrated to America at the age of five, settling with his family in Chicago. In 1924, after six years working in a bookstore, he opened his own place, The Argus Book Shop, first on Wabash Avenue, later moving it to 333 S. Dearborn. In 1940, after relocating to 16 North Michigan Avenue, his bookselling and reputation reached their peak.

Working with four secretaries, two bookkeepers and two cataloguers, the Argus became the most active and famous bookshop in Chicago during the 1930s to mid 1940s. His bookseller catalogue, *Along The North Wall*, and his magazine, *Reading and Collecting,* bear testimony to his natural enthusiasm for books and his flair for writing about them.

Known primarily as a bookseller, Ben Abramson was also a publisher and writer who maintained an extensive correspondence with numerous authors, a collection that filled six four-drawer file cabinets at the time they became a part of the Beinecke Library collection at Yale University. One of his correspondents was Claude Houghton, a British author he first contacted in 1931.

Claude Houghton was born in Sevenoaks, Kent in 1889. At seventeen he began working in an accounting firm and five years later received his formal degree in what would be the American equivalent of a Certified Public Accountant. During World War I he worked in the Admiralty, a position made permanent after the war and one that Houghton would hold for most of his life. After the war he began writing in earnest but for years found that editors everywhere rejected his work, until G.K. Chesterton began publishing his sonnets and lyrics in the *New Witness*.

By 1931, at the time of Abramson's first letter to him, Houghton's situation had changed considerably; he had 16 published books, including lyrics, verse, dramas, novels, philosophical essays and movie novelizations, including *The Big Trail* (1930) starring John Wayne and Marguerite Churchill. Houghton's books were being brought out by established publishers, and some of them, for example, the Penguin edition of *I am Jonathan Scrivener*, sold over 100,000 copies in 3 printings.

Abramson and Houghton maintained a long and active correspondence for more than 20 years. During Houghton's most productive and literary period, Ben championed his work, sold literally thousands of his books from his store, and published three of his works in American editions under the Argus Book Shop imprint—*Neighbors*, *The Riddle of Helena* and *I am Jonathan Scrivener.*

Henry Miller, who in the late 1930s would become another of Abramson's correspondents, was born in Manhattan on December 26, 1891, and raised in Brooklyn. He graduated from high school and completed a brief stint at City College, but soon dropped out and began a whole series of low level jobs before talking his way into a prominent position of employment manager for Western Union in 1920. While he had made some brief attempts at writing, it was not until September, 1924, that he decided to become a writer on a full time basis and quit his job at Western Union. In spite of his good intentions, with the exception of a few magazine appearances and some self-published broadsides, Miller would make little progress in becoming a writer over the next six years. In 1930, deciding to make a final attempt at becoming a writer, Miller arrived in Paris, more determined than ever that it would be here that he would be able to experience success.

During the nine years that he lived in France, Miller published six books, (including *Tropic of Cancer*, *Tropic of Capricorn*, and *Black Spring*), along with assorted broadsides and pamphlets. These writings had been published in relatively small numbers, and while he was receiving critical acclaim from a small but significant group of admirers, he had not received the recognition he had expected. Sales of his individual books during this time were recorded in the hundreds—not thousands.

In January, 1940, at the outbreak of World War II, Miller returned to New York, penniless, with nearly the same anonymity, as before he left. Over the next few months he wrote at a fast clip, *The World of Sex*, two stories that would be published under the title of *Quiet Days in Clichy* and *The Colossus of Maroussi*. In October, 1940, after receiving a small advance from Doubleday Doran, Miller and his artist friend, Abraham Rattner, set off on an automobile journey across America in order to gain impressions that would be the basis for Miller's next book, *The Air-Conditioned Nightmare*. It would be during this trip, in March 1941, that Miller would journey to Chicago, and for the first time meet up with one of his correspondents, Ben Abramson, a man who the year before had generously supported the first American publication of Miller's *Tropic of Cancer* with his agreement to purchase on delivery 500 copies out of a total print run of 1,000. It was also during this visit that Abramson introduced Miller to the works of Claude Houghton.

Miller and Abramson would continue their correspondence for another 15 years after this first meeting. Abramson would publish two of Miller's works: *The World of Sex* (1941, reprinted in 1946) and *Aller Retour New York* (1945). In addition he continued to sell a large percentage of Miller's books that were sold in this country, both under—as well as over—the counter, until his death in 1955.

Houghton's death in early 1961, just months before the Grove Press publication of Miller's *Tropic of Cancer*, prevented him from seeing Miller experience the commercial success and recognition that he himself had enjoyed 20 years earlier. After Houghton's death, Miller would continue to refer to their exchange of letters with fondness and identified them as some of the most personal letters he had ever written. Miller, who outlived both Abramson and Houghton, died in June 1980.

With the exception of Miller's two visits with Abramson, it was the exchange of letters among these three people that would be their only contact—neither Miller nor Abramson ever met Houghton in person. Of all the letters exchanged among them, there was only a single letter which Miller had in his possession at the very end—his letter to Houghton dated January 31, 1942, the original of which Houghton had returned to Miller—at Miller's request—in 1958.

Although the correspondence between Miller, Houghton, and Abramson spanned more than two decades, the exchange of letters forming the cornerstone of this publication transpired between 1938 and 1942, the years when they most directly dealt with Houghton's work.

[Letter from Ben Abramson to Claude Houghton]

December 29, 1941

My dear Claude,

....I corresponded with Miller for many years, although I had never met him, and I was a little surprised to find that his letters were as chaste in word and thought, as some of his books were unchaste in those ways. He stopped in here on his trip around the United States[1], and I found him the most charming and gentle of men, a good companion, who carried with him an aura of kindliness and gentleness. His speech is as chaste as were his letters. I like Henry Miller very very much. He is something of a mystic, and so I gave him *Kingdoms of the Spirit*[2] and *Christina*, and he says in a letter received some while ago,

> "This is just to let you know that I have finished Claude Houghton's *Christina.* I began it in Chicago, you know, and after the first few pages put it aside, having the impression that it was too prosy and pedestrian for my taste. Tonight I picked it up again, always remembering your most vivid account of the story, and determined to see it through. Toward dinner time I ran into Dan, the most interesting character in the book. From then on I couldn't put it down. Well, Houghton interests me. I would like to read some more of his work. Maybe the one about *Chaos*, or else *I am Jonathan Scrivener.* I leave it to you. Give me the most quintessential ones, those which illustrate his philosophy or ancient wisdom. Maybe they all do? He is definitely not a writer in the *sense* of a creator. His style is bold, terse, steno-

graphic, boned down for universal consumption, and yet, he is an aristocrat, a man who, if not to be called an 'initiate' is definitely on the threshold. I like the trend of his mind. I admire his ability to delineate character with hatchet strokes. I like the base on which he erects his edifice. He is too conscious a person to care about 'art,' perhaps. There is no struggle going on. He just tells what he knows clear and clean. You can read him on the upper or lower level, according to your vision. I am convinced that it would make an excellent movie, as I told you originally when I heard you outline the story. In fact, I am going to write Hollywood about it. Now that *Here Comes Mr. Jordan* has proved a success, there is no reason why they shouldn't try *Christina*. Emlyn Williams ought to direct it. Ronald Colman ought to play Dan. When you get around to it, when you have oodles of time, write me a letter and tell me why you like Claude Houghton, so much. I am very curious."

That was written on a midnight Sunday, but undated. On an undated Friday, a fortnight later, he wrote:

"Please send me another Houghton book. The more I think of his *Christina* in retrospect, the better I think of it."

I hadn't sent the book because I was so busy, but now I have sent him several and I await his comments with interest....

Sincerely yours,

Ben

[Letter from Henry Miller to Claude Houghton]

c/o Russell & Volkening[3]
522 Fifth Avenue
New York City, N. Y.
January 31, 1942

Dear Mr. Oldfield,[4]

I have just been through a great experience—the reading of several of your books—and feel compelled to let you know of my indebtedness to you. A year or so ago, on my way through Chicago, Ben Abramson put in my hands your book of essays, *The Kingdoms of the Spirit*. On my return he handed me another—*Christina*. The infection began with this latter. While I was waiting for Abramson to send me *I am Jonathan Scrivener* I came upon a cluster of your books in the library of a young friend of mine, Wayne Harriss, a boy of nineteen who had begun reading you at the age of fourteen while traveling on the Continent. Then I was taken down with the grippe and was able to give myself up to your work unreservedly. It was a most fortunate coincidence, if indeed it is coincidence. I read in quick succession: *I am Jonathan Scrivener, This was Ivor Trent* and *Strangers*. I am about to dip into *Chaos is Come Again* and *Julian Grant Loses His Way*. Meanwhile, as if under a spell of enchantment, I have been to the office of the Viking Press where I consulted the *Book Digest* for the last ten years in order to see what our American critics made of you. And there I came upon a short biographical sketch[5] together with a photograph of you. I feel enriched. I feel happy. And more than ever, I feel free now to tell you some of the things which have come alive in me while reading you.

As I suspected, when I began reading the reviewers, no one seems to have grasped the real significance of your work. I do not mean to imply thereby that I am in sole possession of the clue, but at least I can say this: I accept you unreservedly. I have had a real illumination, reading you. More, I have glimpsed the solution of my own problems. Your characters move in an atmosphere of reality and truth; they not only make a mark upon us, but they alter us profoundly. Each book I pick up seems to have been written for me exclusively, and in making this admission I feel that I am but echoing the sentiment of thousands of your readers.

I do hope that you are still alive and potent, capable of giving us more books. I feel almost as Wrexham did when thinking of the absent Scrivener. It is absolutely essential that you remain alive a little longer. It is not enough that the world recognize your gift—there must be a reconciliation, a union. That which your readers recognize as your special contribution to the world must be made manifest and operative. You answer to a great need, you fill a great void.

I know this must sound almost boyish to your ears and, being an Englishman, perhaps it makes you a trifle uncomfortable. But I assure you there is more than enthusiasm behind my words. I am not a boy; I am a man of fifty, a writer to boot, and beyond that one who has suffered and struggled and searched. In your essays I recognized the sources of your inspiration; in your novels I detect influences of writers and thinkers who have also affected me deeply. In the Scrivener book I feel that it was not altogether haphazardly that you have Wrexham pick up and commence to read *Seraphita*, the only book, aside from *Amiel's Journal*, which you deign to mention among all the interesting volumes in that most mysterious library. I, for whom *Seraphita* had meant so much, would have given anything to hear what you had to say about it (thru the mouth of Wrexham). I was at first disappointed to discover that you had definitely dropped the book. But had I not read *Seraphita*, I most certainly would have—the hint was all-powerful. Subsequently you repeat this performance—but even more cleverly, more effectively. Several times there is mention of certain scabrous tomes hidden away among the other volumes. There is the dramatic entrance of a "low" character, intent upon blackmailing Scrivener. And then there is Francesca, who deliberately takes the volumes from the shelves and puts them under Scrivener's nose. No mention of them seems to me greater than if we were given an inkling of their contents. For myself, it was as though I had swiftly and intensively reread a whole library of Erotica.

Some of your reviewers, I observed, spoke of your dramatic instincts. I was also very much aware of this quality in you. But there is something, it seems to me, which should be added when referring to this facet of your personality—your books begin after the curtain goes down. And by that I do not mean simply that we are thrust back into a realm behind or beyond life, to the realm, I would say, in which we have our being. You have been accused of creating types. True enough. I felt that instantly. But your "types" revive the significance of type: they reveal to us the essential character which is hidden behind personality. We move into the realm of the potential being: we get hints and reverberations of archtypical beings, the real motivators of the drama, which you unroll. And this drama, as I see it, remains essentially the same in all your books, as indeed it remains constant and eternal in life. The discovery of the Self, the reintegration with the Cosmos, with the resultant emancipation of the spirit and a knowledge of the true meaning of Freedom. That is how I read you, at any rate. And that is why I attach such importance to your work.

For some I have no doubt that your books ended most irritatingly at the moment of the great discovery. They are the ones who are hungry for solutions, who will make no effort themselves to come to a solution of anything. They are also the sort who never question the meaning of the word "solution," who would be shocked or disturbed if told that there are no solutions. For them your dramas are abortive. But the intelligent, perceptive, sensitive reader has a very different attitude and feeling with regard to these high moments in which all is concluded and left in suspense. He will go on from the moment of deep conviction and live his life anew. At least, I hope so, dear Claude Houghton, else all has been for naught.

And now may I say something about your drunkards. A great deal of drinking goes on in your novels. Unforgettable drinking, if I may say so. Something utterly different from the sort we encounter in Dickens, Balzac, Dostoevsky and other modern writers of fiction. I am reminded of the story about the man who committed fifty-two murders and how with the fifty-third he discovered that he had murdered the murderer in himself—because the last murder was committed selflessly, was an act of supreme renunciation and hence no longer "murder." You perhaps know the story—it is from India. Well, your drunkards have somewhat that effect upon me. They kill off the drunkard. One realizes that they are desperately drinking to stop drinking. The thirst for life becomes not only caricatural but sinful. It is craving versus desire. The elementals win the day. And the day is followed by an endless night.

I single out this one aspect of the general disintegration all about us because, rightly or wrongly, I imagine it to be highly symbolic of the pseudo-religious spirit which is rampant. I notice how frequently you stress the word "sensation" in your writings. How this corresponds to the complete breakdown of body, personality and spirit. To realize that even in this realm of drink a vast change has come over the world one has to turn, for example to a scene such as Giono gives us in *The Joy of Man's Desiring* where, in a magnificent sensual banquet al fresco, every one becomes drunk as an overflow of life and not as escape from it. But of course here, among the peasants of France, one is still in the realm of the Body—the bodies are all intact. The very title of the book—*Que Ma Joie Demeure!* is significant. I recommend it to you, should you not happen to know it.

I want to run on...It's my chance to pour it out.

There is a great fascination for me in the euphoric aspects of Scrivener, Trent and Grantham[6]—a euphoria which always preludes the bursting of an old level of consciousness. They have their moments of illumination, and we suppose, when we drop the book, that there has been a gain, a foothold won, which will be sustained. Since you mention the words "cosmic consciousness", I take it you are familiar with Bucke's book which has the same title. And I want to ask you, if, as I assume, you have read the book, whether you noticed the paragraph on Walt Whitman in which he deals with the "subjugation" of that new, added faculty. The implications hidden in this paragraph (I do not have the book at the moment and so cannot cite the page) are tremendous, and disturbing. I will put it to you this way...Just prior to reading Bucke's book, unknown to me until recently, I had been immersed in the life and teachings of Ramakrishna, about whom Romain Rolland has written a most exciting book—for Westerners. Subsequently, I made the acquaintance of a disciple of Ramakrishna's—Swami Nikhilananda, who allowed me the privilege of reading the manuscript of one who sat at Ramakrishna's feet and took down his words verbatim. These have been compiled and will soon be published—an enormous tome—by the said Swami, under the auspices of the Ramakrishna-Vivekananda Center here in New York.

This is the point...Between Ramakrishna's behavior and Whitman's there is a world of difference. Ramakrishna went further than Whitman, unquestionably. His illuminations were not only more frequent but they were more sustained and, if I may put it that way, they were more penetrative. Ramakrishna actually said to his disciples, who wished to imitate him, that he regarded it as a vice, his constant living with God. He discouraged them, knowing as he did, that his experiences were not for them. Whitman, Bucke tells us, was *the first man*(!) to live with this added consciousness and harness it, as it were, for the ritual of daily life. He was content to lead the life of an ordinary man, though to my way of thinking, he certainly did not behave like one.

In *This was Ivor Trent* I had the feeling that when Trent disappears with Elsa you were restoring him to the stream of life, as a human being reinforced by a greater vision and fuller powers—and therefore, only therefore, now capable of leading the life of a human being. I wonder if I am right in assuming this? And I wonder, further, if others have remarked on it.

In the case of Scrivener there is something analogous, I take it. He has followed every road to the end, he has found himself in the wilderness, and he returns to the Sanctuary a unified being. He, the greater Self, and Wrexham the little self, unite. It is the Marriage of Heaven and Hell. It is Krishna and Arjuna discovering their identity. But once again, I have the feeling, on concluding the book, that Scrivener will live out his life in complete anonymity, not as a cipher, but as the great ones of this earth who walk among us unknown, unrecognized, seeking to influence us neither by word nor deed but wholly through *being*.

As for Grantham, I feel with him that it was as Balzac said in *Seraphita*—that he had seen the light which kills as well as illuminates. But what a joyous book that is—*Strangers*! What warmth, what a wonderful human glow throughout! Grantham succumbs from well-being, from super-normality, as in Dostoevsky's great work. You may recall the famous colloquy which precedes Kirillov's suicide. I have always thought of it as something unique in literature. It's about "happiness." There is so much I could say about this work of yours, and about the others, but I fear this is getting out of bounds. All I want you to know is that I have got something more than enjoyment from your books. I go about like a child, asking—"Have you ever read Claude Houghton?" I want to put your books in everybody's hands. You are an awakener—and how we dead need to be awakened! Do drop me a line and tell me that you are alive and well, will you?

Sincerely Yours,

Henry Miller

[Letter from Claude Houghton to Ben Abramson]

c/o Lady Stothert
Mount Beacon House
Bath
England
February 11, 1942

My dear Ben,

So glad to get your letter of December 29th....

...you may have wondered why I have "telescoped" answers to your questions—and comments on your news. Well, the reason is—Henry Miller.

Yes, Henry Miller. I want to write about him—and what he said about *Christina*. (By the way, I so hope you have sent him *Julian Grant Loses His Way*. If you haven't, I hope you will.)

I have not read his books, though have of course heard about them. Are they to be obtained in England? You say they were banned in America. What you wrote about the books and what you wrote about the man is interesting. What "got" me is your quotes from his comments on *Christina* is that those comments are criticism. And I don't have to tell you how rare that is. Just praise—or just blame—which are the same thing of course—is negligible. Here are some instances. The book for him meant Dan. The book is Dan. He says my style is "boned down for universal consumption." A good phrase—and a true one. It is. He also says my book can be read on "the upper or lower level." That's what I want. He is the only person who has ever mentioned the "base" on which I erect my edifice. He admires my "ability to delineate character with hatchet strokes." No one else has used these phrases for these penetrations. I hope to God he is right about hatchet-stroke characterizations. But, right or wrong, his comments are criticism—and so they help; help in a creative sense.

So, if Henry Miller writes you again about my novels, I do want you to send it on—all of it. I know you are busy, but don't forget. And I rather want him to read *All Change, Humanity!* But he's probably too busy. Let me know where I can get his books. Either *Tropic of Cancer* or *Tropic of Capricorn....*

As ever, look after yourself—and do write soon.

Claude

[Letter from Claude Houghton to Henry Miller]

Mount Beacon House,
Bath
England

March 1, 1942

Dear Henry Miller,

Your letter of January 31st reached me today—and here I am answering it. That indicates what it means to me. I know I am stupid to write by return. With a letter, as with all thing that are precious to us, one should be an "abstractor of the quintessence," but—there it is—I have to write to you today.....

In his covering note[7] accompanying your letter Ben says you regret that he sent me the extract about my work which you wrote him.[8] Please don't. It was of great help to me. I have read it many times—and shall after, read it again. Inadequate as it was, I hope Ben sent you a copy of what I wrote him about it[9].

And now, before anything else, I want to ask where I can get your books. I understand Ben to say they are banned in America. Can I get them here? Will you be sure to let me know?

No, no, believe me, your letter does not sound "boyish" to my ears. I too am a man of fifty—over fifty—and I am not the traditional Englishman temperamentally. Understanding, in my belief, is a collaboration between two persons whose root experiences are similar. I am always quoting Heine's statement that Literature is a great morgue through which one wanders seeking one's own dead. If certain writers mean much to you (Dostoevsky, Poe, Melville, Emily Brontë, Baudelaire, Ibsen, and many others, and many aspects of certain others—Kafka, Rilke, and so on) then, you have a special type of soul. You, too, in your degree, have been compelled to face certain facts—certain facts with faces of ice; certain facts with a glory that blinds. (Why did I omit Nietzsche—and Spengler, the deeper aspect of Spengler?) Well, your letter tells me that we have stopped long before the same figures in the morgue. You say this—and of course you are right—"I detect influences of writers and thinkers who have also affected me deeply."

Why did I omit Swedenborg and Amiel from my list? Years and years ago, I studied Swedenborg exclusively for about four years. You mention my reference to *Seraphita*, to *Amiel* and—most penetratingly—you relate those references to certain "scabrous tomes" in Scrivener's library. (You remember the bookseller who said to Baudelaire: "Every mystic has a secret vice!!") In a word, you realize the implication—the implications hidden behind hints.

Yes, I begin after the curtain goes down and end when quite another curtain is going up. For instance, every word you write about *Ivor Trent*, at the end, being reinforced by a greater vision and full powers, is entirely true. At least, that is—exactly—what I wanted a reader to feel. But many things in your letter have been mentioned only by you.

I re-read what I have written—and it won't do, because it implied that I knew what you wrote and am commenting on it. That's not the fact. Some things you wrote are entirely new to me. Here's one of them. You find the drinking in my novels different in kind from that encountered in other modern writers of fiction. That's a discovery for me. I'll have to think about it, therefore......I can't help hoping that you read the last part of *Julian Grant Loses His Way.*

It is so long since I read part of *Cosmic Consciousness* I must look up the paragraph on Whitman. I must try to get Romain Rolland's book on Ramakrishna. I am very interested that you met a disciple of Ramakrishna—and read the manuscript of one who sat at Ramakrishna's feet and took down his words verbatim...My ignorant guess is that the supreme task for one who has this "added consciousness" is to harness it. One thing, I think, is certain—all hell will rise to destroy that added consciousness. Surely, that is one of the significances of the temptation in the wilderness—that wilderness to which Christ was driven by the spirit. And, you remember, after the temptations (and what temptations! Dostoevsky is right there) the devil left him "for a season."

No, Whitman wasn't "the first man." He, like us, in our tiny degree, was a liaison officer. Here, he had no continuing city, for he had glimpsed another city—but he did not enter into it. A liaison officer—an inhabitant of the psychic realm, trying to interpret the world, which is either powerless to be born, or is slowly coming to birth, to that world which is dead for him. (Damn it, these aren't the words! Or, I can't find 'em.)

At the end of *Scrivener*, I deliberately had a query suspended in my mind—and I still have. I think Wrexham says in the last part of the book—and the last part, of course, is the most important—that either Scrivener had to go out into the wilderness, to discover his own being, or he had to commit suicide. To be in suspense oneself sometimes creates suspense in a reader!

You see, dear Henry Miller, so often one word is revealing. I am going to choose a minor example from your letter. You refer to Grantham's "super-normality." Everything is in that. Super-normality involves being on a frontier—and so, psychologically, everything is "set" for his crossing that frontier. Heaven grant you are right about the "strange overtone to Kirillov." Yes, unique in literature. And the end of *The Idiot*—and Stravrogin's relation with Verhovensky—and Ivan's with Smerdyakov—and *Notes From Underground*—unique.

How crazy one is! I omitted Blake, and Boehme, from that list on page 1. I will say about Blake that, if you have not read *William Blake and His Circle of Destiny*, published—I am almost certain—by the Columbia Press—it will interest you. And, about Boehme, there is a book, published some six or seven years ago, in America, I think, entitled *The Mystic Will*, which means much to me.

I do not know *Que Ma Joie Demeure!* but you have made me want to read it. Whenever it is to become by, nowadays, is difficult to say.

Another revealing word from your letter. A word, which, of course, has a universe of implications—"elementals."

Now, one or two points, and—for this time—I have done.

The first is—if you see, or write to, Wayne Harriss, will you give him my greeting?

The second is, you can write to me as Houghton, as I am known wholly by that name—or nearly "wholly." Also, this Bath address will stand till I return to London—and that does not seem likely for a considerable time.

The third is—remember to tell me where I can get your books.

The fourth is—I hope you will read (and I hope this for many reasons after reading your letter) my last novel *All Change, Humanity!* Ben could supply you a copy. My last two novels in America were published by Macmillan, but they have turned down *All Change, Humanity!* So, at the time of writing, Harold Ober, of New York, who is my agent, is seeking a publisher. (I have had many publishers in America but not the right one yet.)

I am ending now. Do believe that I am—deeply—grateful for your letter. That it meant much—and especially at the time at which I received it. To "reveal the essential character which is hidden behind the personality." That sentence of yours is true of the work of my masters.

I do repeat that there are many reasons—your "drinking" theory is one of them, but only one of them—why I want you to read *All Change, Humanity!*

Let us write from time to time. When all is in peril, that which was always dear is doubly precious.

You say: "How we dead need to be awakened." You meant: *the* dead.

Bless you,

Claude Houghton

[Letter from Henry Miller to Claude Houghton]

May 10th, 1942
(Mother's Day in America!)
N.Y.C.

Dear Claude Houghton,

Perhaps I ought to say—"Dear Christopher, dear Jonathan, dear Ivor..." Well, I finished *All Change, Humanity!* a week ago or more. I thought I'd let it simmer and settle before giving you my reactions. It's now in the hands of a friend and will slowly go the rounds. Don't be surprised if from time to time you get a letter from a stranger—from some remote place such as Melbourne, Cairo, Pretoria, Timbuctoo. I'm sending your books to the ends of the earth. There are just a handful of people, it seems to me, who will understand what it is all about.

To begin with, this last book marks an advance. Christopher is definitely over the line. In his plenitude he is closer to Scrivener than to some of your other "prototypes." But most curiously, he is the blood brother of N.H.—*The Bright Messenger*. By this time you must have taken note of my allusion to Blackwood's books.

Here's a still more curious analogy....My only criticism of *The Bright Messenger* is that he loaded the book with a host of characters whom we are really no longer concerned with. That applies to your book too. What we want now is to go to Beulah Island and live there! No more dissection and analysis of moribund societies. This last book of yours is savage and ferocious, but *entre nous*, it is a little bit like whipping a corpse. In Paris, just two years before the war broke out, I had the pleasure of sponsoring a book by a young English friend [Lawrence Durrell] of mine (*The Black Book*) which, as the sub-title indicated, was a "chronicle of the English death." There is no need to dwell on this subject any longer. The war is putting the finishing touches to the drama. What is the new life going to be like—that's what we all want to know. Christopher and his ilk have renounced the world. For how long must they continue to be branded as "insane"?

I suppose you have never read *The Letters of the Mahatmas to H. P. Sinnett*? You ought to. It is as though you were reading about the life of the members of an actual Beulah Island. Some few living people have been there. Madame Blavatsky was one. The Theosophical Movement is the result—unfortunately.

But here is a point in common between your book and the real life of the occult brotherhood: the necessity to remain apart from the rest of the world. The necessity to increase and protect the nucleus of a new order of man.

Now and then there are mysterious references to a sortie by one of these strangers from the beyond. (I suppose, in a way, the appearance of the Buddha, the Christ, Mohammed and others could be regarded as an irruption into the world from some remote vantage point. Does not the drama of crucifixion revolve about this fact?

And the great guilt of the world—is it not anchored in this highest form of murder?) But to get back...apparently the only successful issue for the entrance of such a type into the world in that he remain anonymous. In the citation from Vivekanada[10] which I sent you this is stressed in a marvellous way. The implication is, I believe, that through a discipline beyond our wildest imagination, a few men have succeeded in being in and of the world though thoroughly out of it. They have learned how to *radiate* their extraordinary powers without drawing attention to themselves. This to me seems like the greatest gift a man could ask for. And it is in this way that the world is influenced most effectively. No drama is created. And that is extremely important. What a grand waste of spiritual forces has gone into the defense of the great forerunners, entraining finally a behavior on the part of the "believers" absolutely contrary to that of the exemplars. This failure is in great measure due to the character of the "masters" and "teachers" themselves. One should not teach! The truth can only be demonstrated by living it out. As soon as we open our mouths to explain we create confusion. The artist knows this—partially. But at bottom, all art is teaching—is propaganda. And therein lies the tragedy. And the defense of art is wholly egocentric. All the discipline and mastery which the artist acquires is nullified by the desire for immortality. It is utterly unimportant who or what the artist is. An anonymous art would be a step forward—for the artist. (We have had it several times already—and perhaps at its noblest in the erection of the great cathedrals. Europe is only dotted with them whereas in the East—I think of Burma, the city of

Pagan, where in an area of a hundred square miles there were *thousands* of temples!)

If I speak at some length of this, it is because this theme is very close to my heart. For the last few years I have been planning my "escape" from the world. Even while doing so, while imagining the "place" I would elect to retire to, I realized that no such place exists—that it is in the mind and heart, or nowhere. And yet—here is my dilemma—I do find it necessary to need, if only for a while, their moral and spiritual support. Otherwise—and I will be frank—there is the danger of going mad. No, that is not quite it. I shall never go mad, I am sure of that. But I fear that I may be regarded as mad and put with those who are not "mad" but simply crazy. It is rather important to choose which group of lunatics one is going to live with. The mass of lunatics who make up the world are not lunatics in the sense in which we refer to the other two groups. They are more like sleep-walkers—"zombies" of one kind and another. Under a spell, a spell which has lasted thousands of years, too.

This is the plight of the "nascent" being, which D.H. Lawrence understood so well, and which his tragic life exemplifies. I have a better adjustment to life, I think, than Lawrence. But it is an adjustment to the wrong kind of life! I want to get adjusted to myself, to that new self which has been emerging these last few years. When you speak of going into the wilderness—to fight it out with oneself—are you aware that "wilderness" simply means the picture of chaos and confusion which the exterior world presents to one during the moment of rebirth? We think of the wilderness as a solitude, but it is the solitude of the crowd, the sense of being alone and different in the midst of life. The withdrawal from the world is not physical but spiritual. Then, too, it is only when we realize how utterly alone we are that we discover our kinships—and not merely with a chosen few, but with all humanity. Then, I feel, we ought to be able to "rejoin the herd" (I have not read your book of this title yet) and fulfill ourselves without thought of reward or self or concern whether we are understood or affecting the world about us.

You see what problems arise—*after* Beulah Island! I wonder will you engage them. When I say that this last book marks a progression, I mean it in more ways than one. Scrivener was dual... Christopher is single. Christopher takes the leap: Drake follows, and not only Drake, but others. The ecstasy which Trent and Grantham knew has given way to something bigger: joy. Illumination has been followed by action. Faith has become example. A big step. And already, in this book, we have glimpses of the new way of life. Just a peek now and then—but somehow the woman never materialized. Sketchy as Rosa is, she brings us the fragrance of the new world which woman will one day inherit.

Rosas are almost non-existent in modern fiction. And women writers most certainly never give us this type. Blackwood had no woman to match N.H—i.e., while he was "mad." He had to be brought back to earth before he could see the woman he loved. But when he's in the clinic, when she makes love to him, his love, which is cosmic, annihilates her. Here, in this scene, which will remain in my memory as one of the highest in modern literature, one gets intimations of what Dante meant when he created his Beatrice....I find it extremely difficult to talk to women about this subject. If they understand what you're talking about they reject it.

Only the other night I had a discussion with an Egyptian Jew about Mormonism. He knew what plural marriage was from experience in his own country—i.e. he had observed the Mohamedans about him. It didn't work, he said. But polygamy did work with the Mormons—and it was only the fear of their rising power, their success, that made the Gentiles prohibit it. We see something similar going on in the South. The white male is quite ready to have intercourse with the colored woman—it is the white woman who puts a stop to it. She knows she has no chance against the colored woman.

There is no question in my mind but that a high degree of spirituality goes hand in hand with the stud farm. At bottom women would like to be de-romanticized. They are playing this game only because men demand it The fear of promiscuity is just as deep in the male as in the female: the man knows it brings impotence in its trail. But this impotence is psychic, not physical. It's because with each sexual conquest he is obliged to pretend an eternal love; it's the romance that kills him off. Set men and women free and they will be potent at ninety. And what's more they will have eternal love; canalized as it now is, in personal attachments, the current usually burns the socket out. Emotional exhaustion sets in long before sexual exhaustion.

I suppose some of your readers wonder what kind of love life the inhabitants of Beulah Island enjoy. They might just as well wonder what kind of cuisine, what kind of weather, exists there. There's one thing very definite about Beulah Island—anything may happen there. Here in our world all the roads are blocked. The greatest sacrilege is experiment. Wherever you look you see *Verboten*!

[Henry Miller to Claude Houghton-a continuation]

It's now May 24th! A flood of work which obliged me to put the letter aside. Meanwhile I discover more or your admirers. A woman from a book shop in Los Angeles (Campbell's), who gave me an acute and most intelligent analysis of *Scrivener*. Says there was little call for your books there, but among her circle of friends you were well known. You seem to have created little islands of repair—nuclei—which I think is far more important than having a sudden fame. Another admirer bobs up—a rare book dealer. We have a long talk about you. Again I am told you are a dramatist. Every one, of course, admires your portraitures. Universal agreement—they live! They are vivid, unforgettable. One goes on living with them after closing the books. A corollary: most of the characters are too sharply defined, as for the stage. But the principal one, the absentee hero, as it were, approaches the Dostoevskian type, in that you leave about him an aura of mystery, which is the quality of growth, I suppose. One cannot predicate anything about the future actions of Scrivener, Trent, Christopher, and so on. They have been set free, they will act spontaneously. The author does not know everything about them...These are impressions I gather from discussions with your readers.

I think I mentioned having visited your agent Harold Ober. Curious man. Shy as a horse. And inarticulate. Said several people had tried to dramatize your books, but that nothing had come of the attempts. We are all mystified by this. We over here. If ever a man's work lent itself to the theater, yours does. And I should imagine that you would be the best one to do the dramatization. You are a master in this realm. What has prevented this development, can you tell me? A woman in California, whom I succeeded in interesting, wrote me weeks ago that she had written some friends of hers in London—theater people—urging them to do something about your work. I've not heard any more since.

Julian Grant I can readily see being filmed. The first and last sections would go marvelously on the screen, if handled by a good director. I don't know whether you saw a film called *Here Comes Mr. Jordan* (a Columbia picture, I believe), starring Robert Montgomery. A most surprising theme for Hollywood. About a man who had been bought to the after-world before his time—thru a celestial error—and who is brought back to the world to find a new body, his original shell having been destroyed, incinerated. He tried one body after another, and the deaths he goes through and the way he meets each death, most interesting. I saw it three or four times. The author, whom I wrote after seeing the film the first time, I learned was a grocer (an ex-college man), but interested in vaguely occult things. But it took five years for Hollywood to produce the film, and then only at the persuasion of a theatrical producer.

Well, to get back to Ober. He hardly seems like the man to represent you. Struck me as most prosaic. I doubt if he knows what you are driving at. It does seem to me that you should find one solid publisher here who would republish your work and back you unlimitedly. I don't think you've been properly presented to the public. I read Hugh Walpole's encomium[11]—it was mildly intelligent, nothing more. And Hugh Walpole is as dead as a doornail here. I never read a line of his myself, nor do I intend to.

Well, about the drunkards. Douglas Mannering is another. And a most delightful one, I must say. You know these types intimately. I almost suspect you must have been a drunkard once. The lawyer was also superbly, most superbly done. There is always a lawyer or an accountant in your books it seems. This I understand, from the little I have gleaned about your life. If you have led a quiet life, as one is led to believe, then you certainly have extracted the utmost from your experiences. Few writers can tell us so much about a character, in so few words.

Ober made mention of the perennial duality of your heroes. Of course, everybody speaks of this. It is your obsessive note. I wonder do you have any personal explanation to make: For me the rather maddening thing about the off-stage character is your investment of him with unlimited experiences. I would like to recommend your glancing at the Wassermann book I mentioned previously: *The Maurizius Case.* Have a look at that character called Waremme. Notice his explanation for his failure. But notice, too, what a pleasure the author gives in dwelling on his experiences.

And here's a bit of gratuitous criticism I should like to make on my own. It concerns the travel episodes in your books. I felt it first in *Strangers.* Again, when I opened the last book, and was sitting on the Place du Tertre (which I know intimately), I had the feeling that you give us these impressions of a foreign land in a fashion that smacks just a little of the tourist or the guide. Is it that these vignettes are the result of short trips abroad? Or is it that you wish to stick to the purely insular viewpoint of an Englishman? An Englishman abroad? Don't be insulted, please. Again, I noticed that when one of your shady characters is obliged to do a villainous piece of work, you whisk him off to Paris! This gives me a strange, utterly foreign feeling about Paris. The Eugene Sue quality rather—do you see?

Of course I followed the trip which Grantham and Crystal [*Strangers*] made through central Europe with absorbing interest because I covered much of this ground myself in 1928 with one of my ex-wives [June]. And my impressions were very similar to yours. It was my first visit to Europe. I knew only a little German then—no French. I have never written about these experiences—they remain vague, embryonic. Sometimes, indeed, I ask myself if it was really I who walked about the streets of Prague, Vienna, Budapest and so on. These first encounters with foreign worlds are narcotic. I retain only spots of memory. I remember, for instance, a Jew in a ghetto in Budapest, whose sidelocks fascinated me. We talked about New York. I remember the Mathias Kirche up on the bluff overlooking the Danube. And a Roman cemetery and baths some distance outside Budapest. But if I had gone back and lived in these places, if I had struggled there, what a different picture I should have of them? London, for example—I was there twice, a few weeks each time—is terribly vague.

[Publisher's note. Years later when a carbon of this letter was donated to the University of Californina (Los Angeles) Miller added to the last page the following hand-written note: "The rest was in hand-writing. Sorry."]

[Letter from Henry Miller to Claude Houghton]

Hollywood
24 hours later[12]
Thanksgiving Eve
[1942]

Dear Claude Houghton,

I can't tell you how much I am delighted, moved and thrilled by *Hudson Rejoins the Herd*, which I finished a few hours ago. Yesterday, when I wrote you, I had only read thirty pages. I deliberately put it down in order to dream about it. I have been in a state of serenity bordering on bliss for many days now, due to being alone. Last night, on going off to sleep, it was with the thought that (and I have had this often) if the hereafter is a preparation for the next incarnation, and one of memory, and significance (of discerning the pattern, learning the lesson), then I am ready any time. Memory is one of my pet subjects: I am blessed with a remarkable one, in a way. Not the ordinary kind which you are taught to develop—more the Proustian sort, where everything comes up by the roots.

Glancing again at your letter, I see that you ask me to report on Part 1 particularly.[13] Now I am not going to do that—particularly, except to say, that I took it for granted, in reading it, and, as in all your books, I realize near the end how deeply you lay your foundation, how carefully you always prepare the ground. In this book, the themes come off like a fugue. So much so, that at the end, when she cries "Stephen...*Stephen!*" and Hudson answers "Joanna!" you know, you remember, from the opening scherzo that "it's all right"...everything will be fine and dandy. You know that everything begins and ends there, the end in the beginning, as with the mystics. Joined. Full circle. The rose of the cross.

I put it down with tears in my eyes—with extreme elation. Salute! This goes beside *Scrivener* and *Julian Grant.*

Now for the details. I've looked forward to writing you tonight about the book. I hardly know where to begin. As with our *Julian Grant*, this one hits me hard, seems to concern me privately again. More and more coincidences. (How remarkable it is that always, when I have difficulty getting something it is only because the moment was not right. For me things fall into my hand at the right moment. I have learned how to wait. I can wait right through the next ten incarnations, if need be.)

Well, you might never guess, but what concerns me chiefly are Joanna and the Doctor. The Doctor is my pet theme. I wrote you about this once, do you remember? About the anonymous ones.[14] If I have the strength for it, I'm going to give you a most detailed annotation.

To begin with...though I thoroughly entered in the first part, I felt a certain slowness, and then a heavy lag, and began to wonder if you had lost your grip—when suddenly I came to the chapter called "Joanna." From there on I was electrified. (*En passant*—curious that in my letter I mentioned something which you put in the first paragraph of "The Inquest." The line goes..."In every man there is an unknown X...."[15] The second paragraph begins: "Once a man is dead, his destiny is revealed in final perspective."[16] You go on about "the pattern." Here I sat up and meditated. For here is what happened to me, in Paris. Through a meeting with a certain person [Anaïs Nin], through endless talks about my past, I suddenly saw the whole pattern of the past clearly—as clearly as if I were in Devachan, I tell you. And with that came a flood of memories, so great that I was buried under an avalanche. I knew a state of euphoria which lasted easily six months. I reached an emotional peak, and with it the utmost lucidity. That marked a turning point in my life, for it meant that I had accepted the responsibility for all that had befallen me, that I would never again blame the world, that I understood the difference between fate and destiny. That was about 1933 or 1934. If you believe in the seven year cycles, well it was the end and the beginning of the 6th and 7th. A most important period—assuming you have weathered the 33rd year!

It was about my thirty-third year that I decided upon a great change—to become a writer. And to find the woman! (I had been married twice[17], was still with the second one, when it happened.) I found Joanna. (Her name was June, incidentally, and later, when a friend of mine [Anaïs Nin] wrote about her, she used the names Djuna and Joanna for her.) Well, that meeting, the days and months following, were very much like a scene out of childhood. It had all those qualities you dwell on in your book.

I am not going to rehearse my life, don't fear. I want to give you the correspondences. In the year 1927 June, to whom I got married soon as I had divorced my second wife, left me to go to Europe—with a woman [Jean Kronski], a woman whom I loathed and detested. I hated as I have never hated before. It was like the Otto Steele Affair. (My only great hatred). That temporary divorce was a real death for me. Just as you describe yourself slowly and painfully struggling back to life, so might I describe my return to life *during the next seven years.* Up to that point I mentioned, when I saw the pattern of my life clearly and significantly. In that three months when she was abroad I sank to the lowest point. I resolved then that I would write a book about her, about us, which would be immortal. (When I finally began this book, in 1937, I think—*Tropic of Capricorn*—I quoted Abelard in the opening[18]—about no man having suffered as he had, etc. I truly believed I was the only one who had suffered as he, and perhaps more than he!) It will take me to the end of my days to tell the story of my meeting with her and our life thereafter, which lasted until one day in 1933 or 34, in Clichy, where I was living with [Alfred] Perlès, when she suddenly ran away, leaving a note on the table for me, saying that she wanted a divorce. I have never seen her since. I know that she is married to another, younger man (she was very young when I met her), that she dresses like a nun, looks ill, and probably is ill. In most respects she changed completely, on marrying this man—a real volte-face, I mean.

So much for that. Now let me go over the text with you. The clue to the whole drama lies in these words of yours: "The demand we make on life is the exact measure of our potential suffering—and Joanna had demanded much."[19] Like Joanna, June too had entertained the greatest hopes and illusions about a glorious life. Like her, she had been a dancer and had gone on the stage, was extremely beautiful, was generous, reckless, profligate, sold herself over and over (for me). She had a low throaty voice, she was the quintessence of "mystery", and so on and so forth, everything dovetails.

I had always been a child, acted like one, in good and bad ways. Then one day, after heart-rendering scenes between the three of us—June, the other woman [Jean Kronski] and myself—I overhear a conversation between the two of them in which June appears to be defending herself. She is protesting...protesting that she never really loved me, that I was "only a child" to her. I won't attempt to say what effect that had on me—everything will be recorded in due time, in the books, but it was another decisive, shattering moment of reality.

(Shall I add another detail? How, in the very first days of courtship, the thing which melted her, was a tender little thing I had written about my childhood days with Joey and Tony.[20] Let me add that of her childhood I seem to know nothing—it was just a blank—she never could be induced to talk about it. She had *invented* a past to suit herself. I knew it wasn't true. She knew I knew it wasn't true. No matter. In a way I think that her life really began when she met me, that she wanted to keep it that way, wanted to destroy the past...Another detail...we both went to see *Peter Ibbetson* together. It had a tremendous effect upon us. We didn't talk about it. I mention this because there comes a point in your book, where you both "go back"—reminded me strongly of *Ibbetson*.)

Well...another sop about Part 1 for you....I have often said that the first nine years of my life were the deepest, the most beautiful, and the best remembered. At ten, moving to another neighborhood, severing all ties with the place I loved, I seem to have become another person. In the *Black Spring* I tell something about those early years—on the street. I was let loose very young, like a dog—wonderful experience, too. That was my "education"—and a damned good one.

So, you begin to perceive, I trust, my deep interest in this theme, my terrific excitement, my appreciation of every utterance you make?

You say somewhere something to this effect, that if you share an experience with another person you are handcuffed—for life. How well I know that! And how I am shackled! With how many lives! Again: "She multiplies my life mysteriously...." Too true. Again: "every man is haunted by the ghost of his own Potentiality, and though he fears to face it, etc., etc."[21] Yes, yes, yes. "It is fearful how abiding are the real moments of one's life."[22] Amen!

The Joanna chapter. Theme song: "You always want to *understand* everything?" (That was my grievous sin, with June.)

"You always talk as if one has choice in this world." (Me all over. I still talk that way. What's more, I believe it.)

"You'll probe and probe, and analyze and analyze, till there's nothing left." (Might have been taken down verbatim from one of our duets.)

"I felt (Joanna speaking) that everything had been wasted—that I'd made a fool of myself for nothing." (This was one of June's parting shots, and one to which I bow my head.)

"She began to laugh, and she went on laughing as if she couldn't stop." (That laugh of June's used to terrify me—it was like the ground opening up.)

"You won't let anything grow—and you won't let anything die." (Do I know it!)

"You were a kind of god to me..." (The very day she ran away from me June knelt on the street before me and called me "her god.")

"And I read those letters as if God had written them." (June's own words. My letters! What a role they played!)

"My whole life has been an impossibility because of that moment—and that moment was Life."[23] (I could say exactly those words.)

And then the next paragraph, which burns into me like fire, so true they are of the one I knew: "You were generous, Joanna. By God, I believe you were the most generous being ever born...."[24] (Tremendous this, in its similitude, and its truth.)

"She always had the gift of making everything she does seem natural and inevitable. With the result that directly I am alone I feel as if I had awakened from a hypnotic trance."[25]

The next page—waiting for her.[26] Do you know, I think I can and will write several hundred pages on this alone! I've waited through eternities.

Even "the delayed shock"[27] was part of her make-up.

Dr. Bond comes in. "He accepted everything..."[28] "Significant we cannot encounter a being like Dr. Bond without imagining...."[29] (Yes, yes...terribly well put.)

"Perhaps each of us meets one person who is a 'living revelation of the unfathomable.'"[30] (Whose words are these? Wonderful statement.)

"True! You always wanted the Truth, didn't you? And you made your life and mine just hell while you looked for it."[31]

I thought what a wonderful touch to have Hudson muse on how the latch key[32] (one of your infinite latch-keys, by the way) could have found its way back in his vest pocket.

"What the hell does it *mean* to say that most people's lives come to an end long before they die?"[33] (For five years or so this was a sort of melody I used to play with several of my friends. Finally, I wrote a preface to a book called *Bastard Death*, by Michael Fraenkel. Even Aldous Huxley finally got sucked into it. And got out again very urbanely.)

On suffering—the last sentence of the paragraph. Excellent! Follows remark of Sullivan's.[34] (What a thrill I got out of his book on Beethoven! About the quartets, particularly. I never will get over it, it was immense.)

"Poverty, real poverty, is hopelessness—not hardship."[35] (Yes! Thrice yes!)

I thought that a remarkable line, in referring to Joanna—"people who are, strictly speaking, incapable of experience—though they may suffer the tortures of the damned in the actual world."[36]

This also struck me, having felt it often—"To be with her....I become less than myself, and greater."[37]

Then this—you should have put it all in caps: "To me, she is either Child—or Mystery."[38] (N.B. When you do come upon Anna Jahn, in the Wassermann book, remember this...remember about "mystery." Because, I came to the same conclusion about my June as Maurizius did about his Anna. It's desolating, but yet true, I feel. Incidentally, I asked someone to whom I loaned the book to mail it to you.)

"A psychic Ice Age has started..."[39] (By God, I wrote about that ecstatically in *Black Spring*.)

This is really beautiful, and I give you so much credit for having put it that way—hats off! "I believe that, when she left Shardlands, she was Intuition...."[40] (And here is where I make bold to ask, even though it's irrelevant and unwarrantable, but I would so much like to know, believe me—what was the *actual* basis of your Joanna legend? What happened in life? Is it here, at this point, that you merge the dream and the reality, with forbearance, and insight, and tenderness? Would you answer that?)

"I have made a discovery."[41] I can truly say that when, in 1924, I walked out of my job as Personnel Director in the Western Union Telegraph Co., N.Y., swearing I would never again return to work, but would do as I wished, at any cost, I made this same discovery and have lived out the truth of it. And yet, now I am going back—also to rejoin the herd—to take a job, Unless a miracle happens to prevent it—and that is quite, quite possible. We shall see. But I have no fear or loathing about it now. I feel that I am at the beck and call of my own destiny. Everything that happens can only happen for my own good, Perhaps that's something—to know that—to believe it deeply—and be willing at any time to prove it.

Now, about Dr. Bond again. He is a "challenge"[42] you say—not only to you, Hudson, but to the whole modern world. Wonderful. Precisely so. That is what has engrossed me these last few years, just that. And that is Wassermann's marvellous theme, elaborated on, adumbrated, celebrated, raised to the nth degree—in *Dr. Kerkhoven.* So, I *know* you will read it, eventually. (Yes, it will be hard sledding for you, at first, to stomach him....you may have to wallow through a hundred or more pages before it grips you—but it will!)

And now comes the marvellous line. I join hands with you...I bless you! This is it: "I am compelled to believe that he is one of the Unknowns, on whom the world depends."[43] Yes, the Unknowns! This is, or was, one of the greatest discoveries of my life. This changes the whole face of history, when it sinks into you. What a different "Story of Mankind" could be told, from this point of view. India again. What lies behind the Buddhas, the Christs, and all the other great powers of this earth? Who actuated them? Did I send you that quotation from Vivekananda[44] about this? I think I did. Nothing seems truer to me than this, that greater than the Buddha and the Christs, were the unknown ones, about whom nobody knows anything. These men "radiated" power, love, wisdom, and so on. Words, even deeds, were unnecessary. (That takes us beyond Dr. Bond and his ilk, of course. But Bond is a link, a bond. A symbol.)

"No hope—because there is no fear."[45] Yes. Fear! You spoke well on that. In [Otto] Rank you'll get it from every conceivable angle. (He's a pestiferous writer, understand. You'll abominate the style. He was no writer, that's the truth.)

"What, you ask, can Dr. Bond really do in this vast slum of a world?[46] What can he do for the ever-increasing host of *psychic* invalids? What can he do against the Fear of the world?"[47]

This, such a mighty question, you evade answering, my dear Claude Houghton. You dodged it. Or, shall I say, you put the question badly? (For, you know very well, you might just as well have taken Christ or Buddha, as Dr. Bond!) That question can't be answered from the level on which it is hurled—and you know that. Looking at the ever-present mess in which the world finds itself, one could say—"they" accomplished nothing. But that is not true, as you well know. They came, as it is said, "to bring life, the life more abundant." Not to heal the sick and raise the dead. But I don't need to press this home with *you.* You are aware you left this question hanging in the air. Stephen Hudson seems to get no satisfactory answer from his Dr. Bond. Why? (Have I misread some vital point?)

A few more pages later, during the colloquy with Bond, Hudson remarks that not one word of sympathy had escaped his lips. Then adds—"but something deeper than sympathy flowed from him to me."[48] Fine. Then, a little farther down the page, comes the clue because it is the eternal answer of the Sage. "I will do what I can. I always have, and I always shall. I brought her into the world, and I am very fond of her. *But it does not follow that I shall be able to help her....*"[49]

Now here we are, the crux of that Bond problem. The sage has always pointed out that all help must come from within. The Oriental believes this so thoroughly that, as you know, the guru actually puts obstacles in the path of the eager disciple. By the time the enthusiast comes face to face with his Master he has become a master himself. That is their great contribution to practical behavior. *We* lay all the stress on faith. They make faith and action fuse into one. Moreover, they go further....They do not pretend to be able to aid every one. When, after great deliberation, they do agree to accept a *chela,* it is with the understanding that they will be responsible for him *with their own life*! We have never yet come anywhere near this attitude. This was a revelation to me, when I came upon it. It marks the great void between our well-paid analysts (who often destroy people) and the guru of the forest.

A bit more about Bond...In a way, Bond is to be likened more to a Boddhisattva. Here is their pledge—I had once copied into a notebook: "Never will I seek nor receive private, individual salvation; never will I enter into final peace alone; but forever and everywhere, will I live and strive for the redemption of every creature throughout the world."

This, seems to me, can be the only answer to your query, or Hudson's, rather. It removes with one stroke that atmosphere of futility which Hudson spins about Bond's heroic work. It makes it intelligible, instead of mysterious. And by this same logic, with an eye to the "role" which every one is obliged to play here on earth, all behavior, even the most stupid, even the most evil, becomes meaningful. When we see life as an endless drama, we see its meaning. When we sit still and ask why, it becomes meaningless. The "Act"—not action or inaction—gives the clue. In this book, Hudson is another Hamlet, very definitely. Even the nurse knows what he must do. There is a subtle link here between Hudson and Julian Grant. We see it more clearly through their women.

Well, travel on..... A line which made me sit up! "Probably people like Joanna and me eventually do live on the Steeles of the world."[50] Precisely. "If you're lucky."[51] And that is one of those "hand-cuffed" situations which hold a terrible ironic justice. The dreamer and the plunderer. Hand in hand they go, they need one another. Symbiosis. Always the undercurrent of prostitution. Maddening. Haunting. Hallucinating. It can happen just as well with a nation as with a poet.

The end was marvellous. Like all your endings. So Joanna solved the problem. It was like the 53rd murder which the Hindus talk about. The murder that absolves you of all guilt. Not really...not this one...but I like to think of it that way. She laid the ghost, at any rate. Wonderful Joanna! One has to approve of that murder. It was done in love. It was one of those murders which restored the dead to life. The dead Stephen, I mean. I must say, I prefer it to the Shakespearean version. So interesting, always to see how women solve their problems. They are always on the side of life.

Well, enough! As you see, it was a tremendous treat. And don't think that, because of the expansive treatment I gave it, that I put it above the others. I wish you could see the annotations in the margins of your books. It would do your eyes good. But I can't write a letter like this for every book you write. What does Madame Houghton say to all this? And the half-Greek cousin? I wish I could peek through your window. I do hope you're living in a cottage with a low, thatched roof. And there must be a garden! You don't give me any picture of your intimate life. One day I'll come, you'll see. This war won't last forever, by God.

Henry

[Letter from Ben Abramson to Claude Houghton]

October 6, 1939

My dear Claude,

I have reread *Hudson Rejoins The Herd*, and have been able to form a more orderly and sequent opinion of the book.

The hypnotic spell, indefinable, is as strong in this book as in any of your other books. The method of approach to your theme is very effective. The offhand mention, in the opening paragraph, of the lurid incident that led to Hudson's confinement in the nursing home stresses, as no other opening could have, the relative unimportance of that incident compared with the events that proceeded it. As those events come drifting, cloudlike, back to the patient's mind, at first thin and wavering, then taking on greater and greater density, until finally, the whole horizon is black with their shadows, the reader is given to understand that all that was vital in the relationship of Joanna Held and Stephen Hudson and Otto Steele occurred long before Steele shot Hudson in Joanna's flat.

For Hudson, the shooting was significant only insofar as it brought him to a realization of what had led up to it. He did not need to be shot by Steele to know that Steele hated him—hated him impersonally, as a symbol, just as he himself hated Steele. He didn't need to be shot to know that

Steele felt a hopeless passion for Joanna. But he needed to lie at the point of death for weeks to realize what these three, who have known each other since childhood, meant in each other's lives.

Joanna and Stephen, it seems to me, did not stop being children when they grew up. They were impassioned, enlightened children, who expected life to fulfill its promise. The sordidness of Joanna's and Stephen's experiences in the adult world is unmitigated, and, therefore, unreal. In general, all sensitive and imaginative people are disappointed in life. All, in a sense, go in search of their childhood, but not so implacably as do these two. That sought-for childhood is within us, and is rediscovered only at certain rare moments. It is true that those who repudiate their childhood by substituting a pose for a dream are not much good as human beings.

But I believe that you overstate the case when you say that every vital experience in one's life occurs in childhood.[52] This is a contradiction. The experience is not vital, but sterile, if it does not contribute to the full man. The experiences of maturity are not less vital, nor even less keen; they register differently, that is all because the character has been modified by knowledge and awareness. In fact, the experiences of maturity are richer because they tend to clarify the past and complete our memory of it.

As long as Hudson lies in bed, recalling his childhood[53] the narrative is inspired. The smell of snow and rain, the flavor of certain tiny, but all important incidents, the feeling of particular days and places and observations, the look of a house to the child that was born in it, all are marvelously recaptured.

The picture, of course, is idealized, and that is all right, because it is through Hudson's memories that the reader sees it.

The first sight of Joanna is a perfect etching.[54] It was Stephen's first conscious impression of beauty, and it is beauty that he sees in the matter of fact appearance of a little girl. And he first becomes aware of evil in the person of Steele, whom he saw as a small boy.

As you portray him, Steele is the symbol of the self-made millionaire. That he certainly is not. His implacable pursuit of money for the one purpose of buying equality with his betters is as unreal to me as Stephen's and Joanna's arrested childhood. A leading characteristic of the acquisitive man is his pleasure in the game. Steele might be barely credible as an exceptional sort of man, but I don't think you intended him that way.

And I wonder if you intended each character in the book to have a symbolic aura—Dr. Bond, the dedicated soul; Joanna, the votary of life; Stephen, the rebel; and so on.

Otto Steele learns that his money can buy everything except what he wants, but he goes on trying to buy it until death, the only democratic institution on earth, stares him in the face. Those who enjoy the things of the spirit, like Stephen Hudson, cannot understand the acquisitive man's enjoyment of finance. They imagine that he pursues it as the means to an end, and that the end must be the purchase of the things of the spirit.

When Hudson becomes well enough to observe what is going on about him, two sharply contrasted persons press themselves on his consciousness: Dr. Bond, with his gospel of unselfish service,[55] and a disagreeable nurse, typifying the newspaper reading public—a girl who lives and breathes and has her whole being at the key-hole.[56] This nurse is replaced by a pleasant one, whose attractive posterior as she bends over the linen affects Hudson in a way that convinces him that he is getting his strength back. But he doesn't desire Jane herself. His desire is for woman.[57]

He recalls his experiences with the physical part of sex, and finds that none of them meant anything to him emotionally. And for Joanna, none of her experiences had any emotional effect. Physical sex is repeatedly and subtly discredited all through the book.

Joanna and Stephen, between whom there is a strong emotional bond, have nothing to do with each other physically. They form no other permanent alliances, and they always come back to each other at the end of every road. But they are not lovers, and do not contemplate marriage. They are symbols for each other.

I find it difficult to know what to make of such an association. It has no positive element, and it neither grows nor changes. But somehow you have hypnotized me into accepting them as they are.

With such a background, the conclusion of the story is a severe shock. When Stephen learns that he is to be more or less an invalid for life, he goes to say goodbye to Joanna and, with his hand on the doorknob when he hears Joanna say that she had shot Steele, Stephen comes back into the room and embraces Joanna as if he had found the answer to something.

I do not understand this conclusion. I do not believe that a gun can ever solve a human problem. Whatever impediment there was to the complete union of Joanna and Stephen when they were young and ardent and inexperienced was still there, it seems to me, at the end. Either the whole story up to that point is wrong, or the end is wrong.

Steele shoots Hudson; therefore he is hopelessly in love with Joanna: Joanna shoots Steele; therefore she is deeply in love with Hudson: Hudson doesn't shoot anybody, so I don't know how he felt. What's all the shooting for? It sounds like Chicago.

If Hudson's only problem was his ignorance of how Joanna felt about him, why didn't he ask her? How can her shooting of Steele affect his relations with her? There is no indication at any point that Joanna is in love with Hudson or Hudson with Joanna. If it takes homicide to turn the nostalgic into love, the whole thing doesn't make sense. The whole implication is that physical sex, under certain extreme conditions, is justified.

But the arbitrary ending is not the only fault of the book. It is almost a complete recantation of everything that you have written. It is steeped in the mood of emotional pessimism. It is as if a fine creative mind, seized by the spectacle of a world gone mad with destructiveness, were to say—"your values are all wrong, as I have always known, and you are proving it; now that there is more need than ever to oppose the forces of destruction with those of creation, I will prove that I can go to the dogs quicker than you can, and with less excuse, because I know better."

I do not mean that you or any other writer should chirp with shallow optimism, but I do mean that the faith should be kept with their own standards. In your past books you write of the triumph of the human spirit. Absent Jonathan Scrivener dominated the lives of those who knew him; ill and unconscious Ivor Trent did the same; dead Christina was supreme; but Stephen Hudson, alive and kicking, roams all around the world, and can't even hold on to his own spirit, or recognize his woman.

According to Hudson's final decision before leaving the nursing home, there were only two choices left to him and Joanna: either they must live the world's way, or go off the deep end. But there was another alternative. They could go on being Stephen Hudson and Joanna Held.

The idea that their vital lives came to an end with the shooting is a denial of the human spirit. So is the notion that by accepting Steele's legacy to Joanna they would come to accept, in time, Steele's destructive standards. That is to accord as much importance to money as Steele did. If Joanna and Stephen came together at last simply because they were old and tired and lonely, you should have shown your realization of the motive by closing on a tentative, not a final, note.

But this is a good book, and a very exciting one. I cannot expect a novelist to be a philosopher, but he ought to be consistent, and, in this book, you have not been. But you have, as I told you, returned to assume your proper place in a reality that you have created; you have returned to assume a place that no other living writer can successfully usurp.

These impressions were written before I had seen any reviews. I have read only two—Kate O'Brien's in the *Spectator*, and the anonymous one in the *London Times*. I disagree with both, just as the authors of both would disagree with my view; just as, perhaps, you may disagree with my views and inferences. Perhaps a third reading will bring about an alteration of opinion. I'll read the book again sometime next month.

I hope that all is well with you—as well as it can be in a dreary, frightened, uncertain and apprehensive world. Here there has been little change. The news that we get comes from official sources, and cannot be relied upon. Each day, as it brings solutions to yesterday's problems, adds new and more veracious problems...

All my best, dear Claude,

Ben

[Letter from Claude Houghton to Ben Abramson]

c/o Hughes Massie & Co.
40 Fleet Street
London
E.C.4

October 23, 1939

My dear Ben,

Your letter of the 6th reached me on Saturday, and I want to thank you right away for giving thought and time to *Hudson.*

I'm going to answer your letter on broad structural lines, then, if you ever read the book again (which seems a clear impossibility in a life like yours!) you'll see whether or not this letter sheds any light to places that seemed dark.

First of all, in order to give big-scale perspective, I want to make it diamond-clear that Stephen and Joanna commit suicide. The "C.H." note[58] in the front of the book is important. "Recent and tragic circumstances permit the publication of this book." That sentence does a dual job. It "covers" the difficulty of publishing a book which would send Joanna to the scaffold, if she were alive, (and I assume throughout that she is an actual person) but it also hints, by the use of the word "tragic," that the "circumstances" were not normal ones. I believe that to know "posits" the book in a new perspective—and, particularly, the last part of the novel.

So there is no triumph of the human spirit in Stephen and Joanna, unless it be the negative one that neither of them could go on living just for the sake of living. They are lost souls—literally. Magnificent material—just battered to bits by experience.

And now, let's have a good look at the road they traveled.

You say: I overstate the case when I (Hudson!) claim that every vital experience occurs in childhood. Well, Hudson quotes some authorities[59], and could have quoted more, but let us see just how true that was in the case of Joanna and himself.

Take their childhoods, different in every way, but alike in this: *Each was entirely isolated from the actual world.* (Pages 267 to 269, among many others, are important in this connection).[60] Two highly imaginative, impassioned children—cut off by circumstances from the world of actuality—then, suddenly, pitchforked into Actuality at its worst. Joanna—in a "stage" prostitute existence. Stephen—into the war. (The implications of their first meeting, after the war, when they had that row, are very wide and very deep). Their childhood—their vision of childhood—was all they had left. Passionate Innocence, aflame with the wonder, the beauty, the promise of Life. That total surrender of one's whole being to experience which is possible only to a child, or a great artist! (I agree with Hudson there).

What I want to stress is that there were unique circumstances in the childhoods of Stephen and Joanna—parents, homelife, everything. (Bottom of page 69 and most of page 70 are important[61] re: the unique nature of Stephen's memories of Joanna). Not only unique circumstances in their childhoods, but a unique break-away from the shared loveliness of those Shardland days—days magically enclosed in a magic circle. Nothing could recompense them for that loss—not success; not getting the lives they thought they wanted; *nothing*. And, after all, Ben, what the hell does it matter what happens to us so long as the vision of one's heart is a reality? And, when it's not, *can* anything really happen to you? Aren't you just a ghost, haunting the world, arm-in-arm with a dead dream?

I agree that Steele would have found pleasure in the acquisitive game, but, remember, it is Hudson who presents Steele to us. His interest in him is from a very individual angle. Remember, too, that for some time Steele has known he has not long to live. All Hudson's theories about Steele may be wrong. But there is one fact in the situation, and that is that Steele's hatred of Hudson, and his infatuation for Joanna, are strong enough to force him to shoot Hudson directly—he is convinced that Joanna has lied to him—and that she is Hudson's mistress. Steele put a unique value on Joanna.

Who would be a writer? You say: "There is no indication at any point that Joanna is in love with Hudson." Someone else said I had underlined too frequently just how much she was in love with him! Yes, from the moment, pretty early in the book, when Bond asks Hudson if it never occurred to him to marry Joanna. Here's more evidence, given haphazard. She had read Hudson's letters as if God had written them. She had kept that chocolate box. Every sentence she says, in those rows with Hudson (notable in the third visit to the nursing home) is relevant. Jane [Hudson's nurse] knows Joanna is in love with him—hence all her talk about Hudson's "stupidity." All Joanna's hatred of Steele is but a reflex of Hudson's hatred. She tells Hudson that. And, finally, Hudson.....This other person said I had overdone it, and you say there is "no indication." I tell you Ben, it's a hell of a game, this book business!

Yes, if you like, the characters have symbolic significance. Hudson is the Mind—isolated and in rebellion. Joanna is Intuition—isolated, naked, and alone. Steele is the acquisitive Will—isolated and bankrupt. And Bond is the resigned, dedicated Will. Nearer God, if there is God (and Bond isn't certain. He believes "against all the evidence.") And, if there isn't God, then, Bond is a man with a double dose of the gregarious instinct.

You're not far wrong, Ben, when you say that there is emotional-pessimism in the book. I won't hide behind Hudson on that issue. There is despair in the book, which is one reason why the book is of this age. That's a damned penetrating paragraph of yours on page 4 of your letter.[62]

The title, *Hudson Rejoins the Herd*, had about six different meanings for me.

But, you say, that so long as Hudson lies in bed, recalling his childhood the narrative is inspired. "The smell of snow and rain, the flavor of certain tiny, but all important incidents, the feeling of particular days and places and observations, the look of a house to the child that was born in it, all are marvelously recaptured."[63]

Joy, shipmate, Joy! For if I have done that, Ben—if I have made the childhood of every reader (the one he or she had, or the one of which he or she was cheated) if I have made the *vision* of Childhood rise before every reader, then, for me, the book is justified. Let everything else in it be damned bad (add, perhaps, Mr. Jenn[64] is as good as anything in the whole book) I don't care a lot—if the first part really comes off. For I lavished myself on it. So much that, probably, for me, that first part will always be the book. It matters nothing what anyone says, or what anyone could say, I thank God that I wrote that first part. I've never done just that in any other book. And I'd always wanted to do that.

Why did Hudson go to Joanna right at the end? Because he knew then, they were damned—and that they were one in hell, as they had been one in the heaven of Innocence. There was only one more thing that Hudson and Joanna could do together. And that was to commit suicide.

So they did that—together. And went, handcuffed, into the next world.

"Recent and tragic circumstances permit the publication of this book.........."

Well, here's a hell of a letter to send anyone! I'm glad you noted the line about Death being the only democratic institution[65] in the whole world. And Jane's attractive posterior. It would have been a pity to miss that. And, seriously, Hudson's reaction to it provides an ironic commentary on the world's conception of Normality.

I pray that the American edition is doing well. One needs a hand in Europe today....

Write when you feel like it. Thanks again—and a lot—for your letter. Look after yourself.

As ever,

Claude

Claude Houghton and The Novel of The Future*

—Ben Abramson

Dostoevsky said: "Authors for the most part attempt...to select and represent vividly and artistically types rarely met with in actual life in their entirety, though they are nevertheless almost more real than real life itself."

They cannot be known "in their entirety" because the more individual a man is the greater the mystery that surrounds him. But the triumph of their reality lies in this: "that their impression upon literature, as upon life, is indelible. They leave life different because they themselves are different. We remember Dimitri Karamazoff and Jonathan Scrivener, the secret of whose personalities cannot wholly be revealed. We forget the laboratory specimen that can be thoroughly dissected.

A sense of mystery and a gift of prophecy go together. One who apprehends and defines mystery has taken a long step toward solving it. Like Dostoevsky, Houghton has a deep respect for the mystery of human personality and this enables him to give us the present enclosed in the envelope of the future. What man is and what man may become is his sole theme. The external circumstances of man a century or

---

* "Claude Houghton and the Novel of the Future" first appeared in *Reading and Collecting*, Volume 2 No. 1, December 1937.

two from now, whatever they may be, do not detain him. Even though he might give us a glimpse of those circumstances, he refrains, for they would tell us nothing important. Say that a novelist of the early nineteenth century wrote of the future (our present) in terms of airplanes and washing machines. He would have told us nothing of his contemporaries except that they were a people who needed airplanes and washing machines; and he would have told them nothing of us except that we should be able to supply them.

In *Scrivener* and *Julian Grant* and *Ivor Trent* we see the man of tomorrow in the circumstances of today. (This is a reversal of the usual method, which shows us the man of today in the circumstances of tomorrow.) He is strongly conscious of hidden potentialities and impatient of any mode of life that does not take them into account. Living always from this center, he attracts by natural magnetism those half souls who live at the periphery. They can reach the center only through him but they love the symbol more than the thing symbolized, and so his influence often works destructively. Scrivener, having unintentionally transformed the lives of a group of people, escapes, possibly because his god-like function had begun to alarm him; but, although he escapes from them, they cannot escape from him. Julian Grant deliberately uses his power, and, in destroying the souls of others, destroys his own as well. Ivor Trent passes through both phases and goes a step beyond. A sense of impending climax—a climax beyond the one described—hovers in the air at the close of this book. We know what has happened, insofar as incident can explain it, but we do not know (and we never know at the end of any Houghton book) what *may* happen. The situation is an organic thing and its possibilities and ramifications continue to haunt the imagination.

The words "metaphysical" and "idealistic," as applied to novels, have a formidable sound. People forget that these words represent simply the deepest yearnings of their souls—all those dreams and aspirations which the physical world can never satisfy. This vision of something better than we have is the foundation on which Houghton's novel's are built. They are not in the least fantastic; they do not step aside from reality, they step through.

Leonie Villard, Professor of English and American Literature at the University of Lyons, has this to say of Houghton in her recent article *Idealism In The Modern Novel*, which appeared in the *New York Times Book Review*:

> "To Claude Houghton, who is today the foremost, if not the most widely known, exponent of the metaphysical attitude in fiction, one problem only exists: that personal problem the solution of which gives man a clue however incomplete it may be, to the riddle of existence. In such books as *I am Jonathan Scrivener* and *This was Ivor Trent*...love is like the singing of a child in the dark—only a desperate attempt to disguise man's solitude and the utter loneliness of his soul. Through finely conceived incidents, through the varied play of external circumstances, Claude Houghton's novels bring us the finest and most firmly thought-out exposition of the spiritual problem of modern times."

As this critic points out, love plays a minor part in Houghton's novels, although it nearly always provides the illustration of man's struggle toward himself. Sexual emotion is subordinated to his craving for an intenser union, of which the sexual act is a symbol. Because of this preoccupation with the reality behind the symbol, all the love in Houghton, three-fourths of which is extra-marital, seems extraordinarily chaste. One simply cannot associate it with the idea of adultery. Houghton's conception of love is so forcibly and consistently maintained that it seems to outlaw, rather than defy, conventional morality. And it is curious that though the carnal side of love is described with utmost frankness, its appeal is to the intellect rather than to the senses. When a young man in *Neighbors* takes off a girl's rain-soaked stockings, he might have said, as Barrymore did in *Criminal Lawyers,* "I'm not looking at your legs, I'm looking at your soul."

Another curious thing is that although this attitude sounds rarified and ethereal, its effect is quite the opposite. Houghton is not ethereal any more than he is fantastic. Every line that he writes throbs with a strange excitement. If he looks at a girl's soul instead of her legs, he succeeds, by that very act, in making the soul more exciting.

In the destructive as well as in the creative functions of his characters, Houghton's reach for the reality behind the symbol gives an edge to every incident and a significance to every action beyond that which can be logically traced. There is murder committed in *A Hair Divides* and in *Christina.* Both are "crimes of jealousy," as they say in the newspapers. But here we see jealousy itself as the crime, the murders following almost automatically, neither of them consciously planned. The criminal in *A Hair Divides* coveted his friend's genius; the one in *Christina* coveted his own wife. Jealousy in each case completed the man's moral disintegration before ever he lifted his hand against his victim. In the first book we see the potential murderer in the man whose violent rupture with his family came about solely through his need to establish his own superiority; from that it was only a step to the killing of a man whom he recognized as his superior. In *Christina* we see the working of the same destructive force in a man who had to possess his wife nightly to assure himself that she was his. This last is a situation that D.H. Lawrence could have written volumes about—and, in fact, did.

In his descriptions of social functions, Houghton again joins hands with Dostoevsky across the versts. Those monstrous parties, extending sometimes over two or three chapters, are like no parties that have ever been. Resolutely must these authors have put out of their minds all recollections of actual parties, to which people go to kill time and escape from themselves. Nobody goes off so easily at a Dostoevsky or a Houghton party. The fool reveals himself as a fool, and such a colossal one that he touches wisdom; the wise become so profound that wisdom is indistinguishable from folly; rogues fall out, hatreds rise to the surface, and closely-guarded secrets explode; nothing remains as it was.

The party in *Chaos is Come Again* is a picture in miniature of all the chaotic elements in the world today. Anna Petersley, a high-spirited and sensitive girl, is in love with a low, swinish man; Araminta, whose manhood is merely a mockery, exhibits a type of cleverness that makes one wish the world were still full of innocent, inarticulate beasts; a snobbish young evangelist, outwardly, denouncing show, secretly very much in awe of it, is bent on achieving the social success that he officially despises. And there is Isobel Petersley, not a child-wife but a childish one who munches sweets and tries to recapture a glamorous past by reading biographies. There is Keith Petersley, the head of the family, who tries to forget his disheveled world in a half-hearted liaison with an actress. Every Petersley reflects, in his own way, the disorder of the world about him. But when the shock of the crisis comes, each one remembers that he is a Petersley and acts in his true character. And in this affirmation we see the presence of an inextinguishable force for order in the midst of chaos.

In these highly intellectual novels, the intellect comes in for some pretty ruthless treatment. One cannot escape the inference that the final achievement of the intellect is contempt for the intellect. But contempt is too limited a thing to ascribe to Houghton. He does not despise any man's achievements but he has a sense of proportion that shows him the true value of these achievements. In the character of Wrayburn, in *This was Ivor Trent*, he shows us the sterility of intellect when it is divorced from every emotion except the desire to escape from the demands of organic living. At first meeting, Wrayburn seems an amusing and stimulating companion, not only alert to everything that is going on in the world, but able to analyze and evaluate it; at the third or fourth meeting, his friends begin to feel an inexplicable sense of weariness and embarrassment in his company. Something that nourishes and sustains human intercourse is lacking in him. In the character of Trent, on the other hand, we see a man whose vitality affects the lives of everybody he encounters. With Trent, the intellect is simply a tool—the creative force lies in the emotions. A further inference that one might draw from Houghton's books is, that when man, by sheer force of desire, became human, he developed a brain to explain what he had done.

It is true that this attitude is not peculiar to Houghton. He shares it with all great writers. What is peculiar to him is the adventure he makes of man's struggle to be man—the excitement he infuses into the conquest beside which all others are unimportant—and the courage with which he develops, in book after book, the one great theme of which, as Leonie Villard says, he is "the foremost living exponent."

[December 1937]

Preface to *I am Jonathan Scrivener**

—Henry Miller

No people on earth, it seems to me, have been so successful in making life uninteresting as the English. In accomplishing this feat they have become crazed in a way which sets them apart. The unfathomable dullness in which their everyday life is shrouded creates an aura of eccentricity which is most deceptive.

What is typically English? The atmosphere of unreality from which there is no escape. Even abroad the English carry this atmosphere with them. Wherever they roam they are immediately recognizable as lost souls. They move about like distraught phantoms, speaking a language which no one understands, not even their compatriots.

Are they at home in this mock world? Apparently not. Not even seemingly. In their abject forlorn loneliness they give the impression of being condemned to live a life of exile here on earth. Their laughter has an unnatural ring, like something to be apologized for.

In every novel Claude Houghton gives us he creates, or rather re-creates, this atmosphere unerringly. For the most part his characters seem to have been borrowed from another

---

* Written by Miller in April, 1953, while in Bruges. "Preface to *I am Jonathan Scrivener*" first appeared in the French edition of *Je suis Jonathan Scrivener*, published by Corrêa, in 1954.

planet. The most interesting ones are naturally those furthest gone, that is, those who have completely surrendered to the flux. Usually they are derelicts, scoundrels, drunkards, or what Houghton calls, "Bohemians." In short, the dregs of humanity.

Nearly all his novels make interesting film material. To be properly realized they would require the collaboration of a Buñuel and a Painlevé. The suspense created by this super-detective story technique, is uniquely his. It carries over the finale like a prevailing wind that rotates with the rotation of his books. This constant, which is recognizable in all the eccentric English authors, provides the climate of hallucination which has haunted the English scene since the beginnings of her dark and bloody history.

With Claude Houghton this particular English madness—a sort of low pressure madness—acquired a significant edge. Accepting it with the supreme awareness of a sage, he gives it an apocalyptic touch. He seems to say that if there had not been an England it would have been necessary to create one, for everywhere else on earth (except America, perhaps), there exists or persists a modicum of sense, a modicum of reality, which is the despair of devil and saint alike.

The real protagonists of these novels, consequently, are all imbued with the spirit of the coming order. They possess the delightful, refreshing quality of anarchists liberated from the absurd thrall of history. There is not the least hint of madness in them. They have a stark, brilliant quality, a sameness and a lucidity which sets them off from their fellow creatures like gems. Eccentric, grotesque, bizarre they appear to be at times, but always so only in relations to inert lumps of clay or over-active puppets who throng the stage of daily life and who merely assume the roles allotted them by fate! In this humdrum revel of humanity the figures who make a stir in the world have no pre-eminence over fools and simpletons: the priest has no more significance than the criminal or the prostitute, the dictator or revolutionary leader is just as imbecilic as the ignorant or betrayed worker. In a world given over to self-destruction, drama as such is completely nullified. There remain here and there, like stars emerging through inky clouds, a few rare individuals who speak and act as if truly alone, truly alive, and truly aware of the eternality of life.

But perhaps the rarest thing about these rare creatures whom Houghton gives us is their utter detachment. They are interested neither in safety nor salvation: they live in freedom, an achieved freedom, which communicates itself like an intoxicant. They are in the world but not of it; they behave like individuals who have come back somewhere to rest with us a while and hold the mirror up to Nature. They are as much at home in our prisons as in our insane asylum. They employ a fourth-dimensional language which is as remote from Esperanto as the language of Thomas Aquinas is from that of the angels. They have the gift of making themselves understood. But they have also the wisdom to refrain from converting others. They respond to questioning—a torture preserved for the emancipated—only to state and restate the truth which animates them. They act not to impress or convince but to enjoy life. If they have a purpose in carrying on, it is only to reveal that the purpose of life is to live. The privilege of living with such characters for a few moments is a luxury which few contemporary writers are able to give us. Through them we live beyond ourselves in an atmosphere of certitude which is hilarious and lasting. It is a treat for the soul—and without moral benefit. If there is mystery surrounding these new men and women, it is a familiar mystery. We know that they belong to our world, even if not to *this* world. We know that they are not another species of man, but man incarnate, man the Son of God. If we are not at home with them, we are at home nowhere.

Of course they are wholly imagined beings. None of them have recognizable prototypes. None of them exist first as idea. None of them will take their place in our world tomorrow. And if they are not with us now it is because we have excluded them from our consciousness. They are there all the time. The question is not *where* but how and when. And the important thing is not who they are but what they are. Or better yet, simply *that* they are.

Whether Claude Houghton is in agreement with this very personal interpretation of his work I know not. I have had the great pleasure of corresponding with him for a number of years. I have made a confidant of him as I would never think of doing with a fellow American. Each book of his I read seems to convey a personal message to me. More than that, it gives me the courage to continue being mad in my own peculiar way, to continue to be an exile in my own country.

Discovering Claude Houghton*

—by Henry Miller

On returning to America from France I met two individuals[66] who were passionately fond of an English author whom I had never heard of—Claude Houghton. "A metaphysical novelist," he is often called. At any rate, Claude Houghton has done more than any Englishman, with the exception of W. Travers Symons—the first "gentleman" I ever met!—to alter profoundly my picture of England. I have by now read the majority of his works. Whether the performance is good or bad, Claude Houghton's books captivate me. Many Americans know *I am Jonathan Scrivener*, which would have made a wonderful movie, as would some of his others. His *Julian Grant Loses His Way*, one of my favorites, and *All Change, Humanity!* are less well known—more's the pity.

But there is one of Claude Houghton's books—here I touch upon a subject I hope to enlarge on later—which seems to have been written especially *for me*. It is called *Hudson Rejoins the Herd*. In a lengthy letter to the author I explained why this seemed to be so. This letter will one day be made public.[67] What so startled me, in reading this book, was that it appeared to give a picture of my most intimate life during a certain crucial period. The outer circumstances were "disguised," but the inner ones were hallucinatingly real. I

---

* "Discovering Claude Houghton" is an excerpt from *The Books in My Life*, © 1969 by New Directions Publishing Corporation.

could not have done better myself. For a time I though that Claude Houghton had in some mysterious way gained access to these facts and events in my life. In the course of our correspondence, however, I soon discovered that all his works are imaginative. Perhaps the reader will be surprised to learn that I should think such a coincidence "mysterious." Do not the lives and characters in fiction frequently correspond to actual counterparts? Of course. But still I am impressed. Those who think they know me intimately should have a look at this book.

[1950]

Publisher's Note to the Preface for the Miller-Houghton Letter of January 31, 1942

—Roger Jackson

For reasons clearly stated in the Preface which follows, Ben Abramson was impressed with Miller's letter to Claude Houghton and wanted to publish it as *An Open Letter to Claude Houghton.* Miller's approval for this project went to Abramson in the spring of 1946 with Abramson planning on having the book ready for distribution by the fall of that year. Because of financial as well as health problems, the rate at which Ben's publishing was proceeding was going more slowly than expected and two years would pass without the book appearing. In the spring of 1948, when Catalogue 30 of the Argus Book Shop was sent to the printer's, Ben's Preface to the Miller-Houghton letter was included as an advance notice for publication. During the next six months, 150 advance orders for the planned production of 250 copies had been sold, and yet, the book itself had not got beyond page proofs. Delays continued, and the publication was re-scheduled for fall 1951, then spring 1953, though as before, it never materialized. On February 17, 1954, Abramson wrote Miller that publication of his letter to Houghton was delayed indefinitely due to old debts that needed to be paid off, the result of an extended illness.

The original publication was limited to the first letter which Miller sent Houghton, dated January 31, 1942. How many other letters might have been sent by Miller to

Houghton during this year is unknown, with one exception: Miller's letter to Houghton written on Thanksgiving Eve, 1942, which is described as a continuation of a letter started 24 hours earlier. The fate of this earlier letter, most likely a brief mention of his initial reactions to Houghton's *Hudson Rejoins the Herd*, is unknown.

Preface for the Miller-Houghton Letter of January 31, 1942*

—Ben Abramson

Here is a letter from one writer to another writer, but it is more: Here is an appreciation and a laudation; here is a salute by talent of talent.

In 1941 Henry Miller was introduced to the books of a writer new and unknown to him. The new and unknown is sometimes a revelation and in this case it was.

In short: Henry Miller read the books of Claude Houghton for the first time in 1941. He read *The Kingdoms of the Spirit*, and then he read *I am Jonathan Scrivener* and then, in rapid succession, *This was Ivor Trent*, *Strangers*, *Chaos is Come Again* and *Julian Grant Loses His Way*.

I was the first to introduce, across time and space, Henry Miller to Claude Houghton. I put into his hands that remarkable book of essays, *The Kingdoms of the Spirit*. I have led many readers into the unique world of Claude Houghton. In fact, it is one of my avocations and pre-occupations to make his work known to you and others, and you, and you. But I have never felt more proud than on this

---

* This Preface to the Miller-Houghton Letter of January 31, 1942 first appeared in Catalogue 30 of the Argus Book Shop, spring 1948.

occasion when, by giving these essays to Miller, I "granted" him at the same time an experience which he simply had to sit down and write about—6 pages, single-spaced, in fact. For as soon as he had finished *The Kingdoms of the Spirit* he came across by accident a whole cluster of Houghton's books in the library of a friend. He read then all, one after the other, the way a convalescent devours steak and sunshine. He read them and then he wrote to Houghton.

I am printing this long letter of Miller's. I am printing it in book form because I believe it is extraordinary and because I believe it is going to make literary history. We have to wait, especially, for literary history to become history. Posterity, the unknowable element, is notoriously slow at coming forth to assure and reassure and set its seal upon the great ones of our time and earth. But sometimes some of us can feel with a weird, prophetic kind of knowing when the contemporary is going to become the permanent and the enduring. This, as you know, is what I feel about both of these writers. I first felt it about Claude Houghton and I have blown bugles for his name for years. I also felt it about Henry Miller when he was still obscure and starving in Paris. It therefore gives me especial pleasure to combine my feeling for these two unusual and, if I may say so, extraordinary writers, in one book. It is especially rewarding because here is Henry Miller writing in his own inimitable millerose, conveying the essence of Miller to the essence of Houghton.

The letter is a critique and an analysis as well as an appreciation. Claude Houghton gets reviewed as few writers have the honor of being—critics being what they so usually and often are—bored, perfunctory and grudging—who cannot see the ideas for the words, lost in a welter of too much print for too many years.

I could go on and on, but I won't. I want you to have the surprise and pleasure and amazement for yourself. Here is a book you are going to have to have. You want to be in on history, don't you? Well—this is a way. This is a way to be ahead of yourself, and ahead of time. There have been some famous literary letters in the past. Here is a famous literary letter of now. Don't let it be later than you think; the vanguard is already here.

I am printing a small edition of this letter. It will make a very nice little book, I am sure. The price will not be more than $5.00. The number of copies printed will be limited to the number of orders in hand when it goes to press. It will probably be ready during the autumn. Please order to made sure that you will have a copy. You may, perhaps, want more than one copy.

Incidentally, I think you are going to feel, after you have read this extraordinary letter, that you are going to have Claude Houghton's works—if, that is, you are so benighted, my dear friends, as not to own him already. And this doesn't mean just one Claude Houghton. Henry Miller felt the way all sensitive, alert and aware readers feel. (You, too. How can you be less?) One book is such an illumination that it calls for more illumination and then more. One asks for another, and then more, and then more.

If we receive a number of orders sufficient to make possible the inclusion, without added cost, of check lists of the books of Henry Miller and Claude Houghton, this will be done. In any event, since the price will not be more than $5.00. The work, even without the check lists will be, in view of the very small edition, a worthy collector's item and one that will grow increasingly scarce because of its double interest.

[1946]

Henry Miller's Apocalyptic Aspect*

—by Claude Houghton

In this brief article I am concerned with only one aspect of Henry Miller's work, its apocalyptic aspect, and with only one of his books—*The Wisdom of the Heart*. Circumstances necessitate this, but I do not regret it, because I believe this apocalyptic aspect to be the quick of his inspiration.

In the book mentioned, there are two most remarkable essays on Balzac which "lift the veil" because they penetrate to the root of experience from which Balzac's work is derived. Now, many critics apparently believe that imaginative literature comes from the void—this is especially the case with many Shakespearean critics—but Henry Miller knows that great imaginative literature stems from its creator's deepest experience; that every major artist, therefore, has one theme—no matter how many or intricate the variations on that theme may be—and that consequently, there is thematic continuity in the work of a great writer, which is the reason why it is imperative to study his books in chronological order.

So far as I know, Miller is the first to reveal that it was Balzac's "communication with the angels"—as a boy at the College of Vendôme—which informed the whole of his

---

* "Henry Miller's Apocalyptic Aspect" was first published under the title "British Notes" when it appeared in *The Happy Rock: A Book About Henry Miller*, edited and published by Bern Porter in 1945.

subsequent life. Indeed, that incredible life can be understood only by reference to that early and profound experience—that "secret which no one, not even Madame Hansaka, will ever penetrate."

These Balzac essays are examples of Miller's apocalyptic criticism, but other essays in *The Wisdom of the Heart* are supremely important because they are apocalyptic in relation to an apocalyptical age.

> "This is the Apocalyptic Era when all things will be made manifest to us....Nothing will prevent the world from realizing its worst fears—nothing but the elimination of fear itself...The death that has been rotting away in us secretly and disgracefully must be made manifest and to a degree never before heard of."

That last sentence, it seems to me, is the real explanation of what is happening in the world today. Did not a Hebrew prophet say that the flame would consume only that which is already its prey? Miller knows that everything rotten is going to be destroyed. If everything is rotten, everything will disintegrate. If an ark survives this Flood, from that ark will come a new humanity.

> "The complete destruction of our cultural world, which seems more than ever assured by the impending smash-up, is really a blessing in disguise. The old grooves of race, religion and nationality are destined to go, and in their place we shall see, for the first time in the history of man, a community of interest based not on the animal in him but on the human being which had been so long denied. The

fight is between the death instinct and the life instinct."

It is this awareness—this vision of the end—this apocalyptic glimpse of the future—which makes Miller modern in the true sense of that ignorantly used word.

He is of his age because he has *felt* his age. He hasn't just thought and chattered about it. It is heroism, nowadays, to feel. Heroism, because it challenges madness. It is only the man who feels chaos within himself to whom understanding of outer chaos is revealed; and it is only the man to whom this understanding is given who glimpses visions of a new humanity.

There are spiritual paratroopers no less than physical ones. They drop behind the "enemy lines." They battle with principalities and powers. They report the spiritual conflict. We shall learn from them what has happened to the soul of man. Some of them won't get back. Some will send only a word. Some will return with a vision of victory. But their flag will not be easily recognized. It will be a banner with a strange device.

There are spiritual paratroopers, and Henry Miller is one of them.

[London 1944]

A Final Letter: Henry Miller to Dulcie Houghton-Oldfield*

August 29, 1961
London

Dear Mrs. Houghton,

I stopped at the Savage Club yesterday with my friend [Alfred] Perlès to inquire about Claude Houghton and to my great dismay I was informed that he had passed away several months ago. It was indeed a shock to me. Strange too that I should not have heard of it sooner. I have been traveling on the Continent since last September and some of my mail has of course gone astray. I did so much hope to meet him at last after all the correspondence we exchanged. I shall be back in the States the end of this month, but if you ever write to me best to make it c/o Agence Hoffman 77 Blvd. Saint-Michel Paris 5è. I don't know how long I can stand it back home. I am now off for a jaunt through Ireland. I stood before the desk at the Savage Club where I was told Claude Houghton wrote some of his books and I communicated with him silently wherever he is. I miss him.

Sincerely,

Henry Miller

PS. My friend Perlès joins me in expressing our sincere condolences.

---

* Mrs. Claude Houghton

Notes, References and Excerpts from *Hudson Rejoins the Herd*

[Publisher's Note: The reference (ref.) number which is a part of each "Note" identifies for the reader the page of text in this volume where the particular "Note" occurs. Houghton's books are long out-of-print and difficult to obtain. In order to provide the reader with samples of his writing style as well as provide the context in which Miller quoted Houghton, lengthy excerpts from Hudson Rejoins the Herd [HRH] *are provided. Most of the "Notes" from 15 through 65 are taken directly from* HRH. *Bold text identifies specific phrases from* HRH *that are quoted in this exchange of letters. Page numbers listed at the end of each the excerpts refer to the 1939 British Edition published by Collins.]*

1-*ref.* p. 25) In October 1940, Henry Miller accompanied by artist Abraham Rattner, set out in a 1932 Buick on an auto trip across America. The purpose of this trip was to gather impression for what would be published in 1945 as *The Air-Conditioned Nightmare.* The original plan was for Rattner to supply sketches for Miller's text but that was eliminated by the publisher due to cost. Miller first visited Ben Abramson during March, 1941, as a part of this trip.

2-*ref.* p. 25) Writing about this years later, Abramson recalled: "I remember vividly the day I met Henry Miller for the first time, after many years of correspondence. He was staying in Chicago and had nothing to read. He was then in his Zen Buddhist period and I thought he might like Houghton's *Kingdoms of the Spirit.* He had never heard of Houghton. Strangely enough he didn't like the book. I persuaded him to read a few more which he liked very much, and when he brought them back asked for more. He devoured them and then wrote a very impassioned letter to Houghton, a letter which I hope someday to publish." [Taken from an undated document located at the Harry Ransom Humanities Research Center, University of Texas-Austin.]

3-ref. p. 27) Russell & Volkening was Miller's literary agent at the time and provided a permanent address where letters to Miller could be safely sent. At the time Miller's first letter to Houghton was written, he was temporarily quartered in Caresse Crosby's New York apartment at 137 East 54th Street.

4-*ref.* p. 27) Claude Houghton Oldfield was his full name, however, it was simply as Claude Houghton that his books would be published.

5-*ref.* p. 27) This biographical essay by Houghton appears in *Twentieth Century Authors*, edited by Stanley J. Kunitz and Howard Haycraft, published by H.H. Wilson Company 1942 (New York).

6-*ref.* p. 32) Characters from three of Houghton's major works; Jonathan Scrivener (*I am Jonathan Scrivener*); Ivor Trent (*This was Ivor Trent)* and Hector Grantham (*Strangers*).

7-*ref.* p. 37) [Ben Abramson's covering note to Claude Houghton, dated February 6, 1942]: "Dear Claude, Henry

Miller wrote to say he was sorry that I had quoted to you the extract from his letter about your work. He felt it was inadequate and that he should not have written as he did.

I enclose a letter [January 31, 1942] to you which Henry asked me to mail on his behalf. He said he would not mind my making a copy for myself, so I did so. I hope you don't mind.... Ben"

8-*ref.* p. 37) The text of Miller's comments are included in Abramson December 29, 1941 letter to Houghton. See page 25.

9-*ref.* p. 37) Houghton's reactions to Miller's criticisms are included in his February 11, 1942 letter to Ben Abramson. See page 35.

10-*ref.* p. 45) [Swami Vivekananda]: "The greatest men in the world have passed away unknown. The Buddhas and the Christs that we know are but second-rate heroes in comparison with the greatest men of whom the world knows nothing. Hundreds of these unknown heroes have lived in every country working silently. Silently they live and silently they pass away; and in time their thoughts find expression in Buddhas or Christs; and it is these latter that become known to us. The highest men do not seek to get any name or fame from their knowledge. They leave their ideas to the world; they put forth no claims for themselves and establish no schools or systems in their name. Their whole nature shrinks from such a thing. They are the pure Sattvikas, *who can never make any stir but only melt down in love....*

"In the life of Gautama Buddha we notice him constantly saying that he is the twenty-fifth Buddha. The twenty-four before him are unknown to history, although the Buddha known to history must have built upon foundations laid by them. *The highest men are calm, silent and unknown.* They are the men who really know the power of thought; they are sure that even if they go into a cave and close the door and simply think five true thoughts and then pass away, these five thoughts of theirs will live throughout eternity. Indeed such thoughts of theirs will penetrate through the mountains, cross the oceans and travel through the world. They will enter deep into human hearts and brains and raise up men and women who will give them practical expression in the workings of human life...The Buddhas and the Christs will go from place to place preaching these truths....These Sattvika men are too near the Lord to be active and to fight, to be working, struggling, preaching and doing good, as they say, here on earth to humanity...."

—Swami Vivekananda, quoted
by Miller in *The Air-Conditioned Nightmare*

11-*ref.* p. 51) *Claude Houghton: Appreciations by Hugh Walpole and Clemence Dane*, published by William Heinemann, Ltd. 1935 (London).

12-*ref.* p. 54) There is a gap in the correspondence. Miller's letter written the previous day has not been located.

13-*ref.* p. 54) Part 1 includes detailed descriptions of Stephen Hudson's childhood reminiscences. A long excerpt from Part I is given at Note #53 [page 133].

14-*ref.* p. 55) Previously quoted, see Note #10 [p. 107].

15-16-*ref.* p. 56) [Stephen Hudson]: "No man's destiny is revealed until he is dead—for the obvious reason that, so long as he is alive, miraculous or catastrophic change can transform him. It matters nothing how definite the pattern of his life may seem, it is susceptible to instant change. **In every man there is an unknown X,** a mysterious potentiality, which may suddenly manifest itself in a manner totally at variance with his established customs and convictions. The miser becomes a spendthrift: the profligate—a saint. We think we know what we are, but know not what we may become. Who can set boundaries to the Possible?

But once a man is dead, his destiny is revealed in final perspective. The pattern of his whole life is not only defined but instantly seems inevitable, solely because it is no longer subject to change. Directly a destination is reached, every incident of the journey becomes related to it. Nothing is irrelevant. Milestones are transformed into signposts."

HRH, p. 147

17-*ref.* p. 56) Legally, at least, Miller had only been married once—not twice as stated. He was still living with Beatrice Wickens Miller when he met June. Prior to marriage Miller had a multi-year relationship with Pauline Chouteau, referred to in his later writings as the "widow" given that she was old enough to be his mother. It is this relationship that Miller considered his first marriage when writing to Houghton. An essay about Pauline appears in Miller's *Joey: Volume III Book of Friends*, (Santa Barbara, CA: Capra Press, 1979). Hoki Tokuda, prior to becoming Miller's 5th wife in September 1967, said Miller spoke of his 7 wives, four of which were legal. In addition to Pauline, another "non-legal" wife would have been Anaïs Nin, though this writer does not know whom Miller would have considered his third.

18-*ref.* p. 57) [Peter Abelard]: "Often the hearts of men and women are stirred, as likewise they are soothed in their sorrows, more by example than by words. And therefore, because I too have known some consolation from speech had with one who was a witness thereof, am I now minded to write of the sufferings which have sprung out of my misfortunes, for the eyes of one who, though absent, is of himself ever a consoler. This I do so that, in comparing your sorrows with mine, you may discover that yours are in truth nought, or at the most but of small account, and so shall you come to bear them more easily."

Peter Abelard, quoted by Miller
in *Tropic or Capricorn*

19-*ref.* p. 58) [Stephen Held]: "**The demand we make on life is the exact measure of our potential suffering—and Joanna had demanded much.** But, now, the outlines of the actual world, obscured no longer by rosy mists, emerged in all their stark reality. Sooner or later we all discover the Fact-world, that world which goes its relentless way, undeflected by our desires, and unresponsive to our dreams, And, usually, when we do discover it we hasten to join the herd which has one objective and only one:

to snatch all you can for yourself before you tumble into the grave."

HRH, p. 160

20-*ref.* p. 58) The specific essay which Miller's refers to here is not known to exist; however, another essay on these two childhood friends, written nearly 50 years later, titled *Joey and Tony*, was published in Miller's *Book of Friends, Vol. 1* (Santa Barbara, CA: Capra Press, 1976).

21-22-*ref.* p. 59) [Stephen Hudson]: "Does a time come when every man seeks himself—the self that had been the most real, the most alive, the most responsive to the awe and mystery of life? Seeks it everywhere, more and more desperately? I believe that, sooner or later, every man seeks it, for **every man is haunted by the ghost of his own Potentiality and though he fears to face it, in the end he is forced to seek it.** He returns to it—the same way, and for the same reason—as a murderer returns to the scene of his crime.

What did Steele see when he looked at Joanna? Joanna Held, the actress? Or a child? A child in a wisp of a dress at a children's dance? Or did he see neither of these? Did he see himself, lit by the rays of a sun which set long ago, and which he would never see again?

It is fearful how abiding are the real moments of one's life. So abiding that, no matter how deeply they are trodden into the mire, day after day, year after year, they rise more radiant than ever—to crucify and to console. If only these moments could be denied; could be uprooted from memory! If only they would go the way of that great grey host of desultory moments which vanished long since without leaving a single trace in the dust! If one could live with these moments, once and forever, then, one could come to final terms with life. One could accept this jungle of a world, knowing that it is a jungle, and nothing else.

But these moments are immortal, for they are glimpses of the eternal. Was there not a saint who experienced a five-hour ecstasy, and dedicated the rest of her life to meditation on the marvel of that mystery?"

HRH, pp. 206-209

23-24-*ref.* p. 61) [Stephen Hudson to Joanna Held]: "You are linked—always and for ever—with the deepest moment I have known. Perhaps, if I had experienced that moment when I was looking at a sunflower, then a sunflower would be associated with it—always and forever. Nothing you've ever done, and nothing you ever could do, touches *that* Joanna. She's eternal. She's nothing whatever to do with Time. **My whole life has been an impossibility because of that moment—and that moment was Life.**

Almost immediately I went on:

You were generous, Joanna. By God, I believe you were the most generous being ever born! And, because you were what you were, you believed that everyone else was like you. Everything that's happened to you—all your follies, all your recklessness—was caused by the discovery that the world wasn't as generous as you were. Yours was the emotional road—and you went to the end of it. And you went alone."

HRH, p. 237

25-*ref.* p. 61) [Stephen Hudson]: "Worst of all, I have no control over my thoughts from one hour to the next. Sometimes I feel that Joanna's explanation of her attitude at the inquest and her account of her relations with Steele are wholly convincing, but, an hour later, I remember **she always had the gift of making everything she does seem natural and inevitable**. Somehow, when I am with her, she numbs my logical faculty, **with the result that—directly I am alone—I feel as if I had been awakened from a hypnotic trance**. Consequently I vacillate between belief in her and total skepticism."

HRH, p. 238

26-*ref.* p. 61) [Stephen Hudson]: "Each afternoon, about four o'clock, the knowledge that Joanna may appear at any moment excites me to a degree wholly out of proportion to its cause. Directly it is four o'clock, a sense of urgency possesses me. Instantly, I become aware of a number of questions which it is essential to ask, but before I have formulated the first, another rushes into my mind, which is immediately followed by a third. And then, incontinently, I realize the futility of questioning her at all, and I make a compact with myself that I will remain silent during the whole of her next visit, and so discover the subjects which *she* wishes to discuss.

All the time, however, I keep glancing at the clock. Then, as the minutes crawl by, I find it impossible to remain in my chair. I get up and begin to pace the room, telling myself that all this excitement is not related wholly to

Joanna, but is partly the result of being alone for months on end. I keep telling myself that.

Nevertheless, as I continue to pace up and down the room, I make the most childish tests as to whether she will come or not. I say to myself that if she is not here by a quarter to five, I shall know *for certain* that she will not come. But, when the hands of the clock on the mantelpiece point to a quarter to five, I extend the test to five o'clock. And so if goes on. Actually, I do not give up expecting her till nearly seven o'clock. And directly I do finally surrender all hope of her coming, the hours ahead of me seem like a nightmare. I can feel Time, like an invisible serpent, slowly enfolding me in its coils."

HRH, p. 239

27-*ref.* p. 61) [Dr. Bond to Stephen Hudson]: "I should say," he replied, even more deliberately than usual, "that she is suffering from what might be termed **delayed shock**. Like many people who have the capacity of living on their nerves, as the phrase goes, she did not experience immediately the physical effects of the shock she sustained. Possibly, those effects are more serious when they are deferred."

HRH, p. 240

28-29-*ref.* p. 61) [Stephen Hudson on Dr. Bond]: "The man, so far as I could discover, made no demands on life of any kind. Unless a selfless determination to serve can be regarded as a demand. **He accepted everything**—all the folly, all the madness, all the suffering of humanity; accepted it as inevitable, and dedicated himself to combating that inevitability.

As I gaze at him, it seemed impossible that this man inhabited the same world as Joanna and myself. There he stood, motionless, with his gargoyle features lit by those extraordinary eyes, and I began to wonder what had caused him to renounce self, years and years ago, more effectually than if he had entered a monastery.

Incidentally, it is **significant that we cannot encounter a being like Dr. Bond without imagining** all kinds of explanations as to why he is what he is. We invariably assume that some tragedy must have happened to him: the woman he loved must have died, or gone mad. Something of that sort *must* have occurred. We want to believe this. We are determined to believe it. It makes us more comfortable. It enables us to say to ourselves that he is what he is only because he is unable to be like us. We admit all his qualities, but we like to think that they were imposed on him by external circumstances. He did not want to be what he is: he had to be what he is. He would like to have been like us. We argue like this in order to feel comfortable in his presence. Probably dwarfs adopt the same argument when they find themselves confronted by a giant."

HRH, p. 241

30-*ref.* p. 61) [Stephen Hudson]: "Someone once wrote—it may have been Maupassant—that 'Certain chance meetings, certain inexplicable combinations of events—in no way remarkable on the surface—create a deeper awareness of the secret quintessence of life than whole days of ordinary happenings.' He might have said—whole years. And, it seems to me, that certain people by their mere presence make us tremendously aware of that secret quintessence—that sudden and spectral knowledge which reveals everything as strange, unknown, incalculable. Perhaps each of us, sooner or later during our journey through the world, meets one person who is a '**living revelation of the unfathomable.**' For me, Joanna is that person. She always has been, and she always will be."

HRH, p. 244

31-*ref.* p. 62) [Joanna Held to Stephen Hudson]: "**True! You always wanted the Truth, didn't you? And you made your life and mine just hell while you looked for it.** And what was the end of that great Quest? You came back to England, over a year ago because you'd worn yourself out—because you were utterly at the end of things. So you came back to me. *That's* true, isn't it?"

HRH, p. 250

32-*ref.* p. 62) [Stephen Hudson]: "For several days I have been perfectly well. I get up to breakfast—and spend the day pacing up and down the room, or staring out of the window. There is no logical reason why I did not leave this nursing-home a week ago. I have had some clothes sent from my flat, and I have packed and unpacked a dozen times during the last few days. I have even sent the suit I was wearing when Steele shot me to be repaired! It went to the invisible menders a week ago! In one of the pockets I found the **key to Joanna's flat,** and it amused me to try to imagine who could possibly have put it there while I was lying unconscious on the floor of her sitting-room. Anyway, there it was—and it is now in one of the pockets of the suit I am wearing."

HRH, p. 259

33-34-*ref.* p. 62) [Stephen Hudson]: "Most people's lives come to an end long before they die. If you doubt the truth of that statement, take a good look at most of the faces you pass in the street. And it might be instructive to look at your own reflection in a mirror. Look at it with the eyes of a stranger. Anyway, my life ended years ago, and so did Joanna's, and so did Steele's. When the three of us met in her flat last June, it was a meeting of ghosts. One ghost shot another, then shot himself. And the third telephones for the police. That's what really happened.

I know well enough that any one reading the last paragraph might explain: **'What the hell does it *mean* to say that most people's lives come to an end long before they die?'** It means this: A man has died when he has exhausted his inner possibilities. And a nation is dead when it has exhausted *its* inner possibilities. And a culture is dead when it has exhausted *its* inner possibilities. And, once this inner death has occurred, the outward signs are the same—in the man, the nation, and the culture. And the chief of those signs is that each is no longer concerned with vertical values. (I don't use the word, God, because it has been stripped of the last shred of meaning.) The man, the nation, and the culture is concerned only with what they can grab. In their noonday, the god of each has been To-Give. In this decline, the god of each is To-Get. It is the reason why, today, every man is at war with himself—every nation is divided—and Europe is only an armament factory.

And she is terribly afraid of being an armament factory. And she is terribly afraid of ceasing to be an armament factory. Men literally do not know what to hope. Meanwhile, peace rages—war threatens—the fearful becomes the familiar—and a nightmare the normal.

As I see it, it does not matter one damn that the inner possibilities of Steele, Joanna and myself were very different possibilities. The whole point is that we exhausted them long ago. We exploited ourselves to exhaustion. We were, therefore, in our way, representative of the age to which we belong. Everything was exploited to exhaustion long ago. That is why everyone is bewildered. That is why no one has a guess what to do. No, no one! Despite all the bluster, all the boasts, all the planning, all the blackmail—no one has a guess what to do. Every nation has reached the end of its road. And some are so terrified by their destination that they are trying to walk backwards. They emulate the crab—and call it Progress.

But to hell with all that!

Now I am well again, I see clearly that there is only one thing for Joanna and me to do, and that is to realize the facts about ourselves—and then to join the money scramble just as quick as we can. The first fact we have to realize is that we have always been seeking childhood—without knowing it. Far more people than is commonly recognized make their lives hell through seeking the emotions of childhood in the shambles of experience.

A year ago, the extent to which I was enslaved by those early meetings with Joanna would never have crossed my mind even as a fantastic possibility. But you discover the truth about yourself when you return to life from the brink of death. The simple fact is that Joanna and I never recovered from the loss of that innocent world we shared together.

There's nothing extraordinary about that. R.L. Stevenson was not recounting a unique experience when he wrote:

> 'As I go in life, day by day, I become more of a bewildered child; I cannot get used to this world—to procreation, to heredity, to sight, to hearing—the commonest things are a burden. The prim obliterated polite face of life and the broad, bawdy, and orgiastic—or maenadic—foundations, form a spectacle to which no habit reconciles me.'

Joanna and I were not the first, and shall not be the last, to seek lost ecstasy in the gutter. There is always this to be said in favour of the gutter: It is *not* the pavement—and it does reflect the stars.

What you suffer in this world is in direct relation to the demands you make on life. Complex, highly emotional natures make complex and highly emotional demands. With the result that they suffer on more levels than one—and they make slow and painful progress towards the discovery of the true nature of Actuality. In fact, the more sensitive and the more imaginative a person is, the longer that discovery is delayed, for the simple reason that he *cannot* believe the evidence of this eyes and ears.

J.W.N. Sullivan says in one of his books: 'Mozart's G Minor Quintet is the most poignant expression of his angelic anguish at his late discovery of this world's pain' **The discovery was late because Mozart was—Mozart.**

It is the narrow nature which instantly realizes that Smash-and-Grab is the world's actual creed. The sensitive, the imaginative, spend years and years in a psychic No-Man's-Land. They spend years and years between two worlds till, at long last, they cease to be deceived by dreams and visions, and so discover the bleak outlines and the fortified frontiers of Actuality.

What Joanna and I have to do is one of two things: Pack a bag for the next world—or accept the standards of the majority. The secret of most people's 'success' is that they never expect the improbable, and only demand the obtainable. That's the secret of 'pavement' people.

Or, it may be, that everyone you pass in the street has at some time or other dreamed dreams and seen visions. I say, 'It may be,' because God alone knows what goes on in the heart of a human being. God alone knows! But, sooner or later, one by one, they join the huge herd which stampedes after the Great God Grab. Yes, all of us! Even poets—if they live long enough. You may not want anything a lot, but, nevertheless, you have to grab. There's nothing else to do in the Western world. And you've got to get through the day somehow.

Nations in their old age become tyrants—just like old men. Possessions are the only reality. Adventure is over. It is regarded as one of the many fevers and flourishes of youth. It may be that aged nations, like old men, still rendered lip-service to the ideals which once gave life purpose and directions. But it is only lip-service. They may mumble sometimes about the necessity for religion; they may still whisper the words that set their youth aflame. But it is only a mumble—it is only a whisper.

Sometimes, today, in the speeches of public men—or occasionally in leading articles—the old words crop up:

Justice, Peace, Brotherhood. But, already, a moth-ball odor surrounds them. They won't be able to be used much longer. Children will soon be asking what they mean. Eventually, they will appear only in Glossaries. And this will happen because, before long, jungle policies will not need the camouflage of morality. It just won't be necessary. Self-interest will march, alone and unashamed, under it own banner. Ghostly allies will be superfluous.

The fear in the hearts of men today is that only the jungle is real, and that all else—art, beauty, religion, ideals—are dreams. Only the jungle, and the meaningless strife of the jungle, is real. That is the fear which gnaws in men's hearts like an imprisoned rat."

HRH, pp. 261-64

35-40-*ref.* pp. 62-63) [Stephen Hudson]: "Now that I am well, I see the Shardlands days in proper perspective, but the devil of it is that, directly I am with Joanna, she half-hypnotizes me—and so the spell of Shardlands binds me again. But I will be proof against her influence at our next meeting, and I shall tell her we *must* realize that Shardlands was a dream. And that a dream remains a dream even if another shared it.

I am going to show her that everything conspired to make those Shardlands days an idyll—and an illusion. There are several facts she has to realize, and here are some of them.

Her life with her father was, superficially, very different from mine at The White House, but only superficially. What they had in common, and what really counted, is that her father was the dominant influence of her childhood—and my father was the dominant influence of mine. On the surface, these men had little enough in common. One was an actor, an old-type Bohemian, who was always in debt. The other was a man of leisure, a globe-trotter, with considerable means. But they both drank. And that's significant. Joanna's father treated her as if she were a contemporary, and my father treated me as if I were. Both these men were psychic adventurers. Both were "romantics." Both were womanizers. Both were alone, and lonely. Both were dreamers. Both revealed themselves without reserve.

So it is not very remarkable that neither Joanna nor I had the ghost of a guess about the world we were in. She may have known poverty and squalor—she did know it—but it was lit by the rays of her father's romantic imaginings. Held [her father] lived in perpetual expectation of a sudden miracle, which would translate them to Himalayan heights of felicity. He was certain of it. Just as he was certain that Joanna was destined to a great career.

For an imaginative child like Joanna, life with such a being as Held was not squalor and poverty—although they often had wretched rooms, no fires, and not enough food. **Poverty, real poverty, is hopelessness—not hardship.** Held made poverty seem a prelude to Paradise. It is true that he suffered from fits of depression but they were caused by impatience, or a temporary lack of drink, not by despair. Held wasn't a broken man—he was a bouncing man. Now up, now down—but never still. He had the gift of suffusing gloom with glamour, consequently Joanna lived in a fairy-tale world—not in two squalid rooms. And the proof is that, when Held died, she had one dream and only one—to go on stage. Which is another way of saying that she wanted to be like Held—just as I wanted to be like my father.

Actually, of course, this early Bohemian existence determined the pattern of Joanna's life. The life of each one of us is fashioned according to our conception of the Desirable. Joanna's standards of the Desirable were created during those years—and were not renounced when she came into conflict with Actuality. So true is this that I believe—even now—Joanna half expects a miracle will occur, and that the romantic visions of her Bohemian youth will be mysteriously transformed into facts. At any rate, that theory accounts for the fantastic nature of her experiences in the actual world. There are people, and many more than is commonly supposed, whose actions are just caricatures of their hopes, desires, and dreams. **People who are, strictly speaking, *incapable* of experience—though they may suffer the torments of the damned in the actual world.** It is the reason why Joanna seems to have become the ghost of herself—why all she has suffered since she left Shardlands seems no more to her than the fading memory of a nightmare.

In somewhat the same way, when I used to sit as a child in my father's room—that narrow untidy room, smelling of tobacco, with suitcases, plastered with foreign labels, in a corner—*my* standard of the Desirable was unconsciously taking shape. As I sat watching him stride up and down the room, talking endlessly about his travels, my ideal life was being slowly created in the depths of my imagination. When he showed me those photographs of

New York, Vienna, Rome, and God knows where, I stood, imaginatively, on the frontier of a brave new world.

Above all, I was passionately devoted to him. He was a magician who opened door after door in my mind till I was dazzled and entranced by glimpses of the wonders awaiting me when I should be grown-up and free. Without knowing it, a giant curiosity was being created in me—a determination to explore that world of wonder which my father roved at will.

Someone once said that children are intuitively aware of the subconscious activities of their parents. I do not know how far that is true, but I am convinced it is not wholly false. And I am also convinced that children are as deeply influenced, in a negative direction, by qualities lacking in their parents, as they are influenced positively by those their parents possess.

For instance, although Joanna as a child did not realize any of the implications of the fact that Held had numerous 'wives'—realized them no more than I realized the implications of the fact that my father had a succession of mistresses—nevertheless, I am convinced that each of us was influenced, negatively, by these circumstances. They certainly had the very definite effect on me that in all my dreams of the future, and despite my adoration for Joanna, marriage had no place. I saw myself as free, entirely free, wandering over the face of the earth, experiencing everything—and returning at long intervals to tell Joanna about it. That was the future I visualized as a boy and—making due allowance for the huge discrepancy between dreams and facts—that is very much the kind of life I have lived.

Each of us has lived the life we thought we wanted. So, in a way, what Joanna said to me that night in Budapest was true enough. We were sitting on a bench under that huge statue of St. Gellèrt on the Buda side and, having talked about a number of things, she suddenly began to laugh, then she began to cry, and finally she got angry and said that if there were two people in the world who had got what they wanted, we were the two. She went on to say that, as a kid, I had been crazy to travel—and she had been crazy to go on the stage. Well, we had done what we planned—and that's all there was to it.

Remembering that conversation now I feel—as I nearly always do feel whenever I recall anything she has said—that her actual words conflicted with the emotions she was trying to express.

One way or another, I am often forced to think Joanna was a witch in a former incarnation! And probably in a recent one! She has incantatory power. **To be with her**—to remember something she has said—even to think of her—is to be possessed by strange spirits. **I become less than myself, and greater.** She initiates me into a world of queer dimensions. She numbs my logical faculty. She reduces all memories in which she has no share to spectres. She makes her every act, no matter how extravagant, seem natural, normal, and inevitable. She is potent when she is not present. I *know* she is thinking about me now. I half believed that, if I were to turn round suddenly, I should see her shadow flit across the wall.

And she has this strange power over me even now—now, when I am well. All that I have written about her in this manuscript could be dismissed as the fancies of a sick man but, now, I am well again. And her spell remains. I find it terribly difficult to believe that her power is wholly derived from those magical days we spent together at Shardlands. Terribly difficult!

'What is your substance, whereof are you made
That millions of strange shadows on you tend?'

More than any lines, known to me, those express the haunting sense of 'otherness' she created—the sudden thrill of ghostly frontiers.

To me, she is either Child—or Mystery. She is never the notorious Joanna Held.

Nevertheless, my logical faculty frequently revolts against this subservience to her. I tell myself that her power is only a reflection of my longing for my own childhood—that childhood which she shared and symbolizes.

And I tell myself it is high time Joanna and I realized that we are relics. We are relics because we *had* a childhood. Who has one today? A gas-mask dangles in the toy cupboard. In every other room the radio vomits the news of the world. Shardlands? The White House? The winding lane by the brook? The broken-down wall by the little wood? What are these but ghostly memories of a dead dream? We are relics. There is no childhood today, there are only children—miniature adults—most of whom are measured for uniforms directly they are out of the cradle. We are relics—museum pieces. We have no meaning in the modern world. We should make our final bow, and leave the reeling stage.

I, at any rate, would leave it knowing this: Something new in kind is happening to the world. Dictatorships, civil strife, war itself are only minor reflections of something incalculable—Something wholly outside the authority of men. **A psychic ice age has started....**

There are moments when I am certain that I have returned to life only in the way in which a ghost returns—lightly, nimbly, flitting from scene to scene, from memory to memory. Perhaps it is because I have returned as a ghost that Joanna seems to be one. But this is certain: During her three visits to this room—no matter what we said or did: whether we quarrelled, or whether we were silent—I felt that something had come to a long-destined end.

It was somewhat the same feeling that one has during the last night in a house one is leaving. Everything is packed, the surprised furniture awaits removal. The walls are a blank inhospitable stare. A new silence fills each echoing room. The sense of something over forever...the sense of a dying dream....

I can feel her presence in the room now and, as ever, she inspires thoughts which defy reason and outrage common sense. Here is one of those: **I believe that, when she left Shardlands, she was Intuition**—going out into the world, naked and alone. And that therefore, all that had happened to her was inevitable in a world dominated by spectral Reason. In a world so demented that it reduces everything to the level of its own insanity.

And in a strange way—which, I recognize, is little removed from madness—I feel that Joanna, Steel, and myself were essentially one person. One person—mysteriously and fatally divided into three."

HRH, pp. 267-72

41-*ref.* p. 63) [Stephen Hudson]: **"I have made a discovery—I have reached a decision.**

The discovery is that simple and obvious one that I belong to those unfortunate people who never recover from the loss of childhood, and so are perpetually haunted by it. That is the fact, and it has to be faced with all its implications—many of which are none too pleasant. At first it seemed strange that I had to return from the verge of death to make this discovery; but I now recognize that when you are 'healthy'—when you are rushing about trying to scratch up a living—it is easy enough to remain in total ignorance of your real nature. You are so busy 'outside' yourself that you are aware only of your wants, and know nothing of your needs. You almost forget that it is your life you are living. It might be anyone's.

A long illness is rather like entering a monastery. Everything you have ever known suddenly becomes misty and remote. The hours no longer approach laden with demands. Time abdicates. You look down on the life you have lived in much the same way as you watch the mazy windings of a river from the crest of a hill. You know it is your life. You recognize it. But it is outside you, below you. It is yours—and yet you are mysteriously separated from it. To contemplate it may awaken pity or pain, rapture or regret, but all sense of ownership is gone. It is your life, and it is not yours. And, because it has ceased to be yours, you see it with new eyes, and so you discern its essential quality."

HRH, p. 285

42-*ref.* p. 64) [Stephen Hudson on Dr. Bond]: "Odd as it may sound, I have to come to a final reckoning with this old man. That is, I have to fit him into a category. I've got to find a label for him. In the strangest way imaginable, I feel he is a challenge—though I fully realize that this feeling is probably one result of months of illness. Nevertheless, I do feel that **he is a challenge**, not only to me but to the whole of the modern world, and I cannot leave this nursing home till I have reached a final conclusion about this enigmatic man who has visited me here, day after day, week after week."

HRH, p. 286

43-*ref.* 64) [Stephen Hudson on Dr. Bond]: "So, one way and another, **I am compelled to believe that Bond is what he appears to be. That is, I am compelled to believe that he is one of the Unknowns, on whom the world depends.** No monuments are raised to them. They are recognized only by the lonely, the obscure, and the oppressed. God alone knows what actuates them, what sustains them, and the quality of the hope in their hearts—if these is any hope in their hearts."

HRH, pp. 289-90

44-*ref.* p. 64) This quotation from Vivekananda appears in Note #10 [p. 107].

45-47-*ref.* p. 65) [Stephen Hudson on Dr. Bond]: "**Probably there is no hope—because there is no fear.** Their power is derived from the fact that they demand nothing. These are dedicated lives. And they shame the world by their mere presence.

Personally, I find it supremely appropriate that there is something slightly ridiculous in Bond's appearance It is fitting that he should seem grotesque to others. It marks a distinction. Besides, there is something grotesque about him. By all standards, except his own, he's damned near a lunatic.

Also, I find it supremely appropriate that he does not look as if he belongs to this age. He does not belong to it. He belongs to every age, and so he belongs to none.

As to the outward circumstances, which, superficially, explain him and his way of life, I am just not interested. I do not care tuppence whether he became what he is because his wife died, or went mad, or drank herself to death. I am not interested, because I know what happens to most men when tragedy overwhelms them. They do not become Bonds.

So against my will—and greatly against it—I am forced to see in this man one of those great Unknowns to whom—on some world other than this—a secret commission was given, which they execute without regard to any other authority. One of those grotesque Unknowns who, by their mere presence, make the powerful, the pitiless, and the proud seem slightly ridiculous. One of those Unknowns who walk weaponless through the jungle.

On the other hand, no one realizes more clearly than I do the futility of a life such as Bond's. What can this strange-looking man really do against the hosts mustered before him? **What can Dr. Bond really do in this vast slum of a world?** Poverty, suffering, inertia, vice surround him like ever-widening concentric circles. What can he do? He can patch up a body or two, and get it back its weekly wage—if it's lucky enough to have a weekly wage. He can get it back to the conditions that made it ill. He can do that. **But what can he do for the ever-increasing host of psychic invalids? What can he do against the Fear of the world?**

This spectre of Fear, with its thousand heads, which gibbers over humanity—how shall Bond exorcize that? Fear of war, fear of loneliness, fear of losing one's job, fear of disease, fear of death—what can Bond do about these? There is not a fear known to the heart of man which is not exploited commercially today. Fear is sedulously fostered, because there is money in fear—and not only in fear. Politically, the creation of fear is regarded as master policy, because it is the one remaining means of obtaining national unity, Fear handcuffs a man to his fellows. It creates, therefore only a negative unity—but a unity of any other kind revives a fervent welcome today. The creation of fear is a highly organized industry—and one of the very few prosperous ones.

Bond must know better than I do that the great majority of his patients are victims, of one kind or another, of a fear-haunted, inhuman, reeling social system. He must know that. He *does* know it. His eyes know it. And yet, this sublime lunatic goes endlessly on—endlessly on."

HRH, pp. 290-91

48-49-*ref.* p. 66) [Stephen Hudson on Dr. Bond]: "As I stood staring at him it seemed odd that this man had not prefaced or ended his sentence with one word of sympathy—and yet, as he remained motionless by the window, looking down into the Square, I felt that **something deeper than sympathy flowed from him to me.**

"Listen!" I exclaimed. "there are one or two things I want to say to you—things that I couldn't say to anyone else. I'm not taking your advice, and I shall leave England soon, so there is something I want you to do for me."

"I will do anything I can."

"Don't tell Joanna any of this. Don't tell her I am leaving England, or anything else. I shall go, and I shan't come back. I want you to do what you can for her. God alone knows what anyone could do for her—but you will discover it if anyone can. If I felt you were doing what you could for her, I'd know she wouldn't go right to the gutter."

"I will do what I can. I always have, and I always shall. I brought her into the world, and I am very fond of her. But it does not follow that I shall be able to help her...."

HRH, pp. 295-96

50-51-*ref.* p. 67) [Stephen Hudson]: "**Probably people like Joanna and me eventually do live on the Steeles of the world.** In the end—if we're lucky. And, apart from people like Joanna and me, perhaps poets, prophets and philosophers—those who have glimpsed the vision and held the lightning—eventually live on the Steeles. In the end—if they're lucky. Perhaps there is only the Steeles to live on nowadays. Perhaps the Steeles own everything. Perhaps everyone, everywhere, is living on the Steeles—so you have to come to terms with them, or perish. For a few years you defy them, then you become one of their remittance men. In the end—**if you're lucky....**"

HRH, p. 306

52-*ref.* p. 70) [Stephen Hudson]: "It is impossible to overestimate the effect of overwhelming experience in childhood. A child and only a child—or perhaps the greatest of artists—is capable of complete dedication to joy or sorrow. The effect of a vision of beauty—a moment of terror—a glimpse of evil—remains inoperative through life. I believe that the lesser artists are perpetually tormented by memories of their lost childhood, and that is why they are half children. Whereas the greatest artists remain children, no matter how white their hair may be. And that, perhaps, is the reason why they continue to see and feel life uniquely—why they can reveal a new-minted, freshly created world which is half-reality, half-dream."

HRH, p. 77

53-*ref.* p. 70) [Stephen Hudson]: "A long, rambling, white, two-storied house, half hidden by trees, set far back from a little lane that winds through meadows and woodlands till, eventually, it rises to meet the road which climbs to a sleepy town—with one straggling street either side of the market place.

The White House!

I am returning to it. Like a ghost, I am stealing along the winding lane towards the sudden turning which gives a glimpse of the old white house gleaming among the trees. In that house I was born. There I lived till I was fourteen. It is twenty-seven years since I looked at it for the last time through a mist of rain. Although my body is lying on this bed, my spirit steals along the winding lane through the cradled peace of the countryside. I see a child hastening towards me. And that child is myself. His arms are outstretched: mine are outstretched.

I can see the sudden turning, by the fallen tree near the brook. The sun is shining, birds are singing, lovely lacy clouds float across an azure sky. But the aspect of the scene changes at the whim of memory and, almost immediately, the landscape dwindles to barren autumn, and I see Joanna and myself seated on the fallen tree by the brook, watching little flotillas of faded leaves floating past on the swift-running stream.

The house rises before me like a vision—the house that exists only for me. If my father or my mother could return to it, each would see a different house. Other memories would wave to them from the windows; beckon in the drive; call from the hidden garden. Other hopes would dance for them in the sunlight. Other fears would sidle up in the twilight. This was not the house in which their eyes were unsealed to the strangeness of life. They were not children here. This house was only a house to them—not the universe. It was not here that they discovered the sun, moon, and stars; the slow dance of the seasons; the rain, the wind, and the snow—the awe, magic, and mystery of things. They could never see the house that rises before me now. No one has ever seen it—no one will ever see it. For me, it is not a house. It is the beginning of time; the birth of the world; the dawn of consciousness. It is Childhood. And I have returned to it.

I can see the long circular drive with its overhanging trees; the slender columns of the porch; the shallow stone steps leading to the white front door. How still everything was on summer afternoons when the shadows of inter-lacing branches were stencilled on the ground! How wild on winter nights when the wind roared through barren boughs!

The door opens and I stand in the square hall, facing the winding staircase, remembering how slowly my mother ascended those stairs, frequently stopping to rest—and how my father leaped up them two or three at a time.

On the left, is the door of this room. That long narrow untidy room with books and riding whips lying about, and a pile of suitcases, plastered with labels of foreign hotels, in the corner near the window. Surely no one will ever know rest in that room. I have stood in the hall a hundred times, listening to him talking to himself as he paced endlessly up and down. Again and again I have been startled by a sudden laugh from that room and, when ever I entered it, I felt I was in another room in another house—a strange room in a strange house.

Again, I stand outside the door. But no sound comes from the room—no restless pacing, no sudden laughter.

Then come memories of other rooms in the long, rambling house; of eerie twilight corridors; of attics filled with ghostly forgotten things: a stuffed white owl, a painted chest, a tarnished sword, a wickerwork woman, a rickety rocking-horse. Then come other memories of wet afternoons when I wandered through these echoing attics, stopping to look quickly over my shoulder—the rain pattering on the roof like fine shot, the wind moaning round the house like a spirit in pain.

So many empty echoing rooms! Doors past which I often had to creep noiselessly—the white doors of my mother's room, near the top of the staircase. White, mysterious doors, which would open unexpectedly to reveal a nurse with a finger to her lips, or an old doctor with puckered features, shaking his head. So many tortuous passages with steps leading up or down to deserted rooms, each with its own individual smell, each with its own unique silence! So many rooms, musty with memories, in the long rambling house!

But there is one of which it is necessary only to think for the door to open of its own accord—the nursery with its diamond-shaped windows looking down on the drive; the nursery with whitewashed walls covered with fantastic drawings, done by my father in many-colored chalks. I can see the high guard in front of the fire; the cuckoo clock over the blue mantelpiece; the gay furniture; the green woollen monkey hanging by one hand from the picture-rail near the door. I can hear the bough of the oak tree outside tapping the window-pane on winter evenings when curtains were drawn and a leaping fire sent shadows scampering over the walls. I can hear the drowsy murmur of summer afternoon—the sound of a lawn-mower in the distance, the hum of a bee, the sudden song of a bird. I can see a young red-apple-cheeked nurse, with laughing eyes and hands on her hips. I can hear her say, "Do you think I've nothing else to do but play with you? You'll be the death of me before you're done."

I can see my bedroom—a long white room and, at the foot of the bed, a dark five-fold screen on which is depicted a many-colored bird like a stork. I can see the window through which I used to climb on hot breathless summer nights—to hurry to a secret meeting with Joanna in the grounds of an overgrown estate about a mile down the lane.

The White House!

It rises before me, the house that exists only for me—the house that is half-dream, half-reality.

I am stealing through the hall on tiptoe towards the big sitting-room. I am standing by the French windows, looking out at the 'first' garden. Three stone steps lead down from the terrace to a velvet lawn sentinelled by trees. On the left, I catch a glimpse of the stables, half-hidden by a great oak, and, beyond the lawn, I can see the gap that leads to the 'second' garden.

(I put down my pen and close my eyes....I have travelled all over the world and, presumably, when I leave this nursing-home, I shall wander again over the face of the earth. But never have I known, and never shall I know, the exultation, the winged delight, the rapturous release of my whole being which overwhelmed me as a child when I went through that gap into the second garden.)

I cannot describe it. It is not *a* garden, it is as many gardens as I have memories of it—and I have numberless multiplying memories of it. Shall I describe it in spring, summer, autumn, winter—at dawn, noon, twilight, night? Shall I tell of it when I was three...four...five...six? Shall I remember it when thunder echoed and rolled and crashed, and lightning laced the sky? Or when it was mute and motionless under the magic of snow?

It does not exist for me as a clearly defined remembered whole. In one mood, I see the row of red hawthorns to the right of the gap, flanking the path that leads to a wood. In another, I am running along the grassy path to the left of the gap, with Shirley poppies of every hue on either side. Sometimes I wander in the great flower garden; sometimes in the kitchen garden; sometimes I see only the meadows beyond, great green meadows, lit by dandelions—the song of soaring larks falling from a blue sky. Sometimes I stand and gaze at the view on the left, across a deep valley filled with orchards and gardens, to the far-distant hills. A chalk-pit gleams in the sunshine; the white smoke of a miniature train trails like an ever-lengthening banner. Sometimes I wander on and on through the meadows till I stand on the verge of an overgrown 'precipice.' Midway from its bulging flank hangs a half-uprooted pussy-willow which blossoms in the spring. Clinging to boughs and tufts of grass, I climb to the bottom of this ravine, then follow a grassy path leading to a lane. Nearby, is a small musty-smelling sweet shop, where Joanna and I used to go. When you open the door, a bell starts to jangle—and it is still jangling when you leave....

I know this long rambling white house, with its stables, gardens, and meadows, is only the background of a dream—dreamed once, long ago but, till I was seven, it was the universe."

HRH, pp. 19-23

54-*ref.* p. 71) [Stephen Hudson on first meeting Joanna Held]: "I stole on tiptoe to a narrow staircase, was beginning to ascend, when I looked up—and stopped dead.

A girl was sitting sideways on a low window-sill half-way up the stairs. Her face was in profile and she evidently had not heard me for she did not move. I do not know how long I remained motionless looking up at her. I only know that as I stood there, a new and terrible knowledge slowly transfixed me.

People speak of Beauty as if it were a fireside dream—something pleasant and companionable—a kind of lucky accident. It is nothing like that. It is holiness and terror—a marriage of heaven and hell. It exalts and annihilates simultaneously. It is ecstasy and agony—a glimpse of a shadow of God. And it matters nothing what occasions the first realization of this double aspect of Beauty—whether it be a polar landscape; racing seas of foam under the moon; or a child of eleven in a wisp of a dress, sitting on a window-sill.

As I stood gazing up at her I did not know whether she was dark or fair. I did not even know whether she was beautiful—although she had inspired a vision of Beauty itself. Eventually, after what seemed an eternity, she turned and saw me.

For nearly a minute we gazed at each other. She looking down, I looking up. Then someone called her. She slipped off the window-sill, came down the stairs, passing so near to me that her dress touched my hand.

Directly she had gone, I did not believe she was real. But, real or not, I knew that so long as I lived I should remember what had happened to me on those stairs in the Crown Hotel.

I walked down the corridor as it I were in a trance. I knew that something had come to an end—that something incalculable had begun. I have felt that certainty three times in my life, but never so profoundly as on this, the first occasion."

****

"I only remember odds and ends of our conversation. I know I took her programme and scribbled my name down for every dance she had left. She had given the last to Otto Steele, and I wished he had secured any rather than the last.

I remember little of our conversation because of the overwhelming effect of her presence. This was not caused simply by her appearance. Probably there were prettier girls at the dance—I don't know, there may have been—but everything about her was unique—her dress, her shoes, her voice, the movements of her hands, the way she bit her underlip to restrain a smile.

God knows she was attractive enough! She would have compelled attention anywhere with her lithe figure, perfectly shaped head, dark curly hair, and her extraordinarily intense eyes. But her attraction did not depend on physical attributes. It seemed wholly independent of them. Had she been plain, she would have been unforgettable. It was the vitality, her love of life, the whole sweep and surge of her great generous nature which made her unique. And it was her total unawareness of this—her instinctive assumption that she was like everyone else—which made something in you bow down to her.

Everything in me responded to her, responded so deeply that I scarcely heard what she said. I ceased to be aware of the Crown Hotel, the music, the dancers—everything. It did not matter whether we sat out, or danced—whether we spoke or were silent. A sense of fulfillment possessed me. But simultaneously, I realized how alone I had always been without knowing it, and that henceforth loneliness would cease to wear a mask."

HRH, pp. 45-46, & p. 48

55-*ref.* p. 72) Previously quoted at Notes #28-29 [p. 114].

56-*ref.* p. 72) [Stephen Hudson]: "For the first time since I came to this home, over three months ago, I no longer dread the presence of anyone except the doctor. Also, the thought of conversation no longer appalls me...

Thinking this over, I am convinced that this change is caused chiefly by the departure of 'Maudie.' Since she went, I have realized how deeply I loathed her—so much so that now it is difficult to believe she was just one single separate person. I feel that a whole crowd of objectionable people have gone out of the room for good. Perhaps that is why I like Jane so much. In a very different way from 'Maudie,' she too seems more than one person. She's everyone who is young, vital enthusiastic—everyone who has not discovered the world. There's still a hint of the child-like in her clear features, untroubled brows and blue eyes. And that is attractive when one is tired, terribly tired, of the battered branded faces one sees everywhere.

When she is with me, I forget three-quarters of what the world had banged and hammered and rammed into my head—and that is precisely what I want to forget. There are people you are glad to identify yourself with and Jane is one of them. To identify yourself with her is to catch glimpses of distant desirable things. She is **a key-hole** through which you peer into the bolted room of your youth. I envy her and I pity her simultaneously. If you are not like Jane, life is not worth the living. And I would not be like Jane for all the gifts of all the gods."

HRH, pp. 108-9

57-*ref.* p. 72) [Stephen Hudson]: "They tell me I shall not be able to get up for some weeks. But the fact remains that I have three good reasons for knowing I am better.

And one is that, yesterday, I smoked my first cigarette since I came to this nursing-home. It made me feel giddy, so I did not finish it, but, within an hour, I lit another. The second reason is that, last night, I suddenly discovered I wanted a stiff whisky and soda—and I had one. And the third and most important reason is that, this morning, when Jane was bent double sorting the linen, I was interested in the somewhat exuberant curve of her posterior, which her attitude emphasized. Very interested. So interested, that I suddenly felt the gnaw of desire—the old familiar ache of the senses.

It's evident, therefore, that I am better. I'm on my way back to humanity.

Incidentally, it's necessary to explain that I did not desire Jane—as Jane. Not in the least. **I lusted after woman**—not *a* woman—just Woman."

HRH, p. 133

58-*ref.* p. 76) "Recent and tragic circumstances permit the publication of this book—which was written by Stephen Hudson in a nursing home.

The manuscript has been in my hands for some months—and sheds new light on one of the most remarkable inquests of recent years.

There is one minor point which may be worth mentioning.

Scrawled diagonally in the margin of the first page of Hudson's manuscript, is this quotation from one of Keats' letters to Reynolds:

'Lord! a man should have the fine point of his soul taken off to become fit for this world!'

Whether Hudson intended this quotation to serve as the text of his book, I am unable to say."

[initialed] C.H.
HRH, p. [5].

59-*ref.* p. 77) [Stephen Hudson]: "The first is from Baudelaire: 'Genius is but childhood recaptured at will. For the child, everything is *new:* he is always *intoxicated.* Nothing bears a more striking resemblance to what is called inspiration than the joy with which forms and colors are absorbed by the child.'

The second is from Poe:

'The teeming brain of childhood requires no external world of incident to occupy or amuse it.'

And the third is from Romer Wilson:

'The years of early youth, the time of the dawn of consciousness, are the most important of a man's life. I hold that by the age of twelve a human being has experienced both the highest and the lowest emotions of which he is ever to be capable.'"

HRH, pp. 77-78

60-*ref.* p. 77) These pages in Notes 35-40 [p. 121].

61-*ref.* p. 78) [Stephen Hudson]: "It is important to explain why my memories of these holiday meetings with Joanna during those three years have a unique character. Most memories are vague, because the actual events from which they are derived were so intimately connected with other irrelevant events that, with the passing of time, they merge into a general mist through which we get glimpses of lovely sunlit scenes. Few events occur in isolation. They happen in a jostling crowd of other events which hem them in and therefore become associated with them. It is the reason perhaps, why some very old people stare endlessly at the past, seeking shapes in the mist.

But my holiday meetings with Joanna during these three years were entirely isolated from other events and other people. We might have been alone on a desert island. Consequently my memories of those meetings are in a category apart. They are like memories of a dream. They have no context but their own.

They surround me now—as I lie on this bed in a nursing home. They surround me like a whirl of dancers, each of whom carries a mirror, in which some incident of those far-away days is reflected. I watch scene after scene in bewildering succession—a spring morning in an orchard: Joanna riding a white pony in a round field: a summer house in early autumn: a fallen tree by a brook: a five-barred gate in the moon-bewitched beauty of a July night. Scene after scene after scene—lit from a sudden instant—then disappearing into darkness.

But if the settings of these many meetings emerge only to vanish, the image of Joanna is permanent. Lesser memories may troop in and out of my mind, like tourists, but she is constant in her niche. She is so clear to me that I feel she must be somewhere—just as she was then—and that one day I shall find her."

HRH, pp. 69-70

62-*ref.* p. 79) [Ben Abramson to Claude Houghton]: "But the arbitrary ending is not the only fault of the book. It is almost a complete recantation of everything that you have written. It is steeped in the mood of emotional pessimism. It is as if a fine creative mind, seized by the spectacle of a world gone mad with destructiveness, were to say—'your values are all wrong, as I have always known, and you are proving it; now that there is more need than ever to oppose the forces of destruction with those of creation, I will prove that I can go to the dogs quicker than you can, and with less excuse, because I know better.'"

[October 6, 1939]

63-*ref.* p. 80) Stephen Hudson's early childhood reminiscences are printed at Note #53 [p. 133].

64-*ref.* p. 80) [Stephen Hudson]: "Till I was seven my isolation was almost complete. In the first place, I was an only child. In the second, everything relating to my parents was unusual, and although, naturally, I knew none of the facts, I was vaguely aware that our mode of life was different from that of others. The servants knew this of course—and children know everything that servants know. Not that they ever told me anything directly, but their half-humorous acceptance of sudden changes in domestic routine plainly showed that they had learned to regard the unusual as the normal.

These changes were frequent and were caused either by my father's abrupt departures and unannounced returns, or by the state of my mother's health, which frequently made her a prisoner in those rooms near the top of the staircase, and which sometimes allowed her to become a social being again for a few months. One result was that visitors would be fairly frequent, for brief periods, then the house would be deserted for weeks on end.

Till I was seven, all this affected me very little. I was remote and perfectly content in a world of my own—a world made magical by another, of which I had sudden and frequent glimpses.

All sorts of disparate and quite trivial things gave me intoxicating glimpses of this "other" world. Sometimes I felt I had entered it and would never return to the world of actuality. Quite trivial things effected this miracle: a monotonous tune from an old musical-box; summer rain on the leaves of the oak tree outside the nursery window; the garden, ghostly with snow, under the moon. Often, if I gazed long enough at the colors in my glass marbles, or at a ball of tinsel, I seemed to enter this "other" world, leaving my body in the familiar one.

This "going out of yourself," as an old Irish nurse called it, happened frequently till I was seven. I had the curious conviction that certain people were inhabitants of this "other" world, and only visited the everyday one on rare and special occasions. I was quite certain that this was the case with **Mr. Jenn**, for everything concerning Mr. Jenn was very mysterious indeed.

He was a piano-tuner and used to come to the house at long intervals but with unfailing regularity. I would stand at the diamond-shaped window in the nursery, waiting for him to appear at the end of the long drive. He was a wisp of a man in rusty black clothes, with a big head and unruly white hair. He walked in a furtive kind of way, almost on tiptoe, and always carried a little shiny black bag. Sometimes he would stop and wave his hand in a very peculiar way as if he were dismissing invisible companions.

He always arrived exactly at midday. I often used to hide in the hall to watch him take off his big black hat and his funny little overcoat. He never spoke to the maid who opened the door. He merely nodded his big head up and down and smiled in a strange gnome-like way. Then he tripped off to the drawing-room and, soon after, the most remarkable sounds came from the piano. I couldn't make them out at all. Sometimes I thought Mr. Jenn was torturing the piano and sometimes I thought he was having a most extraordinary conversation with it—a conversation in which Mr. Jenn made the piano repeat certain of its remarks over and over again as if he simply could not believe what the piano was saying.

I always insisted on taking Mr. Jenn's lunch to him. I used to open the door and carry the tray carefully to a little table near the piano which was exposing its elaborate insides for Mr. Jenn's inspection. Directly I appeared, he swung round and nodded, looking intently at me with his queer little black-button eyes. His whole manner suggested that I knew he wasn't real, and he knew it too but neither of us would tell any one else. Sometimes he would point at his lunch, wrinkle up his forehead, and bite his under lip, as if he were trying not to laugh at the ridiculous notion that he needed human food. All the time I was with him I felt I was in that "other" world—that fantastic world which was somehow so much more real than this one.

But Mr. Jenn belonged to that "other" world. I was certain of it. When I stood at the nursery window, watching him depart I was convinced that directly he was out of sight he would either cease to exist or would turn into someone entirely different. He pretended to be human just to please us, and because he was friendly with a mysterious being shut up in the piano. That is why he nodded his head and smiled—and never spoke.

It was years before I discovered that Mr. Jenn was a mute..."

HRH, pp. 24-26

65-*ref.* p. 81) [Stephen Hudson]: "'The world passeth away, and the lust thereof.' Maybe. But, for many, the world is little but misery and, often, the lust thereof flickered out long ago. But, for the rich, the famous, the proud, the world holds much and, often, the lust thereof is the very breath of their being. It is small wonder, therefore, that they recoil in horror; small wonder that they revolt when Death—**the only democratic institution in the world**—confronts *them*, in precisely the same way in which, sooner or later, it confronts the failure and the fool."

HRH, p. 201.

66-*ref.* p. 93) Ben Abramson and Wayne Harriss.

67-*ref.* p. 93) Miller's reference is to his Thanksgiving Eve, 1942 letter and not his first letter to Houghton dated January 31, 1942. It was Miller's first letter to Houghton which Ben Abramson had planned on publishing in a small edition.

On The Works of Claude Houghton:

Critical Reviews
and
Brief Summaries

General Comments

"In each novel the method of presentation is the same. There is a slow accumulation of significant details, significant conversations, significant scenes. These are piled up by the skill of the author as into a card house of extravagant height. Then, on the final page, a door opens, a cold draught comes whistling in, the edifice collapses and you turn from that slight, important wreckage to face for the first time the real problem of the book—the stranger who opens the door and lets in that dramatic draught...

I know of no writer of today who can so surely recreate for us the actual physical sensations which attend a mental conflict. It is an enviable gift, Houghton's power to involve the reader so completely in the tale told that it becomes for him an extension and an explanation of his own life. Defoe had that gift, beyond all other English writers. He could make his Everyman-reader identify himself by a thousand trivial, irrelevant details with his Everyman-hero, till he actually became Crusoe, living lonely on an island at the world's end...

I am aware that nothing is so hurtful to an author as over-praise. Nevertheless, I would like cautiously to suggest to the modern reader that Claude Houghton can exercise for his benefit an art very similar to Defoe's. He too can persuade his everyman by a thousand convincing details that he and the hero are embarked on the same adventure. But the island to which Houghton lures his hero and his reader is the island of spiritual isolation, and everyman experiences there adventures of the spirit."

—Clemence Dane

"I believe Claude Houghton to be one of the most interesting and one of the most important novelists now writing in England. With none of his contemporaries can one compare him—his odd mixture of reality and fantasy, his gifts of drama and of philosophy, his unusual and significant and courageous themes, his natural aptitude for narrative, this last one of the rarest of gifts among novelists today. The important thing is, I think, his uniqueness, and he has come into his full power at just the time when the English novel needs such a man as he."

—Hugh Walpole

"Each book of his I read seems to convey a personal message to me. More than that, it gives me the courage to continue being mad in my own peculiar way, to continue to be an exile in my own country."

—Henry Miller

"In Claude Houghton's work you have come to expect not only an unusual and fast-moving story, but one with its hidden excitements or seeming touch of fantasy, the significance of which may not be apparent until you have reached the last page."

—*Sunday Times*

"Claude Houghton—the foremost, if not the most widely known, exponent of the metaphysical attitude in fiction....His novels bring us the finest and most firmly thought-out exposition of the spiritual problem of modern times."

—*New York Times*

All Change, Humanity!

"Set against a background of the international scene between May, 1938 and May, 1939, *All Change, Humanity!* is a brilliant and incisive criticism of our social structure in an already doomed world—a world in which there must be a complete change of heart or inevitably the people must perish. It is concerned with a family of many ramifications. The Mannerings had been thrown "out-of-gear" by a scandal, caused in 1907 by the wife of John Mannering. For three centuries they had been tradition incarnate, but this book is concerned with them after they had broken with this tradition. In this family are revealed, all the problems and perplexities, all the perversities, stupidities and subterfuges of the inter-war years. Here is shown a society living on the brink of catastrophe, and knowing it, despite endless chatter about 'Safety First' and 'Security.' Here is depicted a family wholly dependent on tradition, which had become traditionless. Here is revealed, in dramatic terms, this family's descent towards catastrophe.

All Change, Humanity! is a book of many characters, of many situations, of many settings. It is a novel of intrigues, of desperate endeavors to outwit malevolent destiny, of passionate relationships and icy antagonisms. This book depicts three aspects of the modern world:—the parasitical Mannerings represent the static-minded, intent on the preservation of their privileges; Sir Michael Mannering represents the patriotism of an England roused by vital challenge; and Christopher Bell represents the promise of a new world."

—Collins Publishers

Chaos is Come Again

"The party in *Chaos is Come Again* is a picture in miniature, of all the chaotic elements in the world today. Anna Petersley, a high-spirited and sensitive girl, is in love with a low, swinish man; Araminta, whose manhood is merely a mockery, exhibits a type of cleverness that makes one wish the world were still full of innocent, inarticulate beasts; a snobbish young evangelist, outwardly, denouncing show, secretly very much in awe of it, is bent on achieving the social success that he officially despises. And there is Isobel Petersley, not a child-wife but a childish one who munches sweets and tries to recapture a glamorous past by reading biographies. There is Keith Petersley, the head of the family, who tries to forget his disheveled world in a half-hearted liaison with an actress. Every Petersley reflects, in his own way, the disorder of the world about him. But when the shock of the crisis comes, each one remembers that he is a Petersley and acts in his true character. And in this affirmation we see the presence of an inextinguishable force for order in the midst of chaos."

—Ben Abramson

"Had Emily Brontë written *Heartbreak House* the result might have been rather like Mr. Claude Houghton's richly invective *Chaos is Come Again*."

—Norman Collins

"Mr. Houghton has an acute and ruthless mind....It is a book full of nervous energy, and delightful ingenuities."

—Frank Swinnerton

Christina

"*Christina* is the story of a man, Peter Brand, whose whole being is undermined by retrospective jealousy. To read this book is to witness the disintegration of a powerful, successful, dynamic personality. But it is much more than that. This novel is conceived and projected in the terms of a tense drama. Brand's search for his dead wife's lover leads him into strange places and into stranger company. One dramatic scene follows another as Brand pursues his quest. Mr. Houghton's dialogue and characterization have been praised again and again. Both achieve new conquests in *Christina.* It is probable that the character, Dan, will find a permanent niche in the reader's memory. Two worlds confront each other in this book: the world of 'success' and the world of 'failure.' It is a tense, dramatic narrative of modern life moving to an overwhelming climax."

—Collins Publishers

Hudson Rejoins the Herd

"Claude Houghton tells us that this book was written by Hudson in a London nursing home, after he had been shot by a famous financier, Otto Steele, in the flat of a notorious actress, Joanna Held. For weeks Hudson was on the frontier of death. For months he is isolated from the world in a nursing home. This book is the record of his return to life. Slowly, from that long illness which is like a monastery where Time abdicates, he gropes his way back into contact with the outside world; comes back from a vast interior universe to rejoin the herd of the living.

And the most overwhelming experience of that return journey is—childhood. So it is not the last tragic meeting between him and Joanna and Steele which confronts Hudson on his way back to the world. It is the *first* meeting of the three of them—years and years ago, at a children's dance in a country hotel. From that first meeting are built up the lives of Steele, Joanna and Hudson. And always, luring the reader on from page to page as Hudson picks up the threads of the story, there is the tantalizing question: What was the true story, the inner story, of that shooting drama in Joanna's flat?

The question is as tantalizing to Stephen Hudson as it is to the reader. His illness had cut him off from the world. He does not know any more than the reader, what happened after Steele attempted to murder him; nor does he know the subtleties of Otto's relationships with Joanna; nor can he understand Joanna's strange behavior. Some tremendous truth, the key to the whole story, is hidden from him, though he is scarcely aware of this, as he discovers one fact after another. Till finally the truth—and the whole truth—about that last tragic meeting is revealed: a truth for which Stephen Hudson was completely unprepared.

But over and above the ever-moving and ever-developing story, this book has a unique evocative quality. It brings your childhood back to you. It magically dispels everything which Experience has battered and banged and hammered into you. You glimpse that heaven which 'lies about us in our infancy.'

This book not only evokes your most precious memories, but it makes you travel the winding road which leads to and from them."

—Collins Publishers

"What is it about Mr. Claude Houghton's work which gives it so marked an individuality of its own? It is not any peculiarity of style; it is not the unusual course which a story of his will generally take. It is rather a kind of hidden excitement produced in the reader's mind by the conviction that something is there, subtly elusive, possibly fantastic, even if it may be wholly baffling, which only at the right moment will be revealed for what it is. So at any rate it is with *Hudson Rejoins the Herd*. It is a strange story, but a strangely attractive one, and, as you expect, very beautifully told."

—Sunday Times

"Mr. Houghton always attacks his problem with a spiritual curiosity so eager that whatever he writes has the quality of urgency. I find it disturbs me, but also it stimulates me."

—John O'London's

I am Jonathan Scrivener

"James Wrexham, in *I am Jonathan Scrivener*, was lonely and at loose ends. He longed for something that would give point and purpose to his life. He takes a job offered to him by a stranger, a man he has never seen. In order to interest his employer, Jonathan Scrivener, he represents himself as a man who has seen through the triumphs of life, who is weary of worldly distractions and wants a life of study and reflection. Scrivener, who really is such a man, entrusts him with a great responsibility.

In Scrivener's absence, Wrexham lives in his house and works at cataloguing his library. He meets Scrivener's friends and discovers what a strange influence the man has been on every life he has touched. Unfolded before his eyes is the record of such an interesting and colorful life as he had imagined for himself. But who is Scrivener really, and what are his thoughts and feelings about all this? Can it be that Wrexham in that letter of self recommendation had really been describing Scrivener, whom he had never seen."

—Ben Abramson

"When *I am Jonathan Scrivener* first appeared in 1930, this brilliant experiment in soul searching caused such critics as Lewis Gannett to greet it as a novel of first importance even though it was classed as a mystery.

'The book,' said Mr. Gannett, 'has moments of painful penetration, as, for instance, the hero's remark that he was subject to "the sublest form of pride—that pride which evades action in order to avoid failure so abject that it would have to be admitted. And the mystery of the character of Jonathan Scrivener, slowly distilled from the characters of his friends is strangely exciting."'

Each year new readers have been discovering the novels of Claude Houghton, this fascinating romantic mystic 'who insists that there are more spiritual worlds than this one in which we live and that it is a man's chief business to discover his relation to these worlds.'"

—Doubleday Doran

"From its first sentence we are as helplessly held as if Mr. Houghton were the Ancient Mariner."

—*Country Life*

"So remarkable is truth is this novel, that I cannot understand why it is not universally known and admired."

—Hugh Walpole

Julian Grant Loses His Way

"This book might be construed as a parable of man's tragic misuse of the powers and possibilities of life. But even apart from any such significance, it is a magnificent story. Julian Grant is represented as a brilliant and personable young man who comes into a fortune and decides to use it as a means of exploring avenues of life which have hitherto been closed to him. He is engaged to marry a young girl named Dorothy. She might have been any young girl named Dorothy, but to Julian she has been, up to this point, a symbol of his life's aspirations. Then he meets Stella Farquhar, a very attractive young married woman whose personality and mode of life seem to promise a richer and more varied experience than he could have with Dorothy. He deserts Dorothy and enters into an intimate love affair with Stella. He meets her friends, and discovers that he can dominate at will whomever and whenever he chooses. Stella continues to be for him the one person of importance in this newly discovered world, but she is also a symbol of his conquest—a point of departure rather than an end in herself.

Julian has a brief love affair with a woman whom he does not care for but wishes to humiliate. He succeeds too well. Stella hears about it. She is shocked by his brutality and leaves him. This makes clear to Julian what is happening inside himself. He knows what his perverseness is costing him, and he makes an effort at amendment by writing to Stella a full confession of his feelings and motives. Enough of his old character remains to enable him to write this letter, but the dominant strength of his acquired character makes it impossible for him to post the letter. His relationship with Stella goes on, but its original meaning is lost. His wealth remains to him; he is young and his life is still varied and interesting. But the meaning has been drained out of everything, and in the end he finds nothing but emptiness.

The novel is susceptible of various interpretations. You can select for yourself the point at which Julian Grant lost his way. He inherited a lot of money, but wealth did not corrupt him. He deserted his first love, but if he had married her instead, he might still have met Stella and felt toward her as he did. He had brilliant gifts which might have been turned to some valuable form of work, but work can be just as much a drug as idleness. It is clear that Julian Grant ceased at some point to be Julian Grant, explain it how you will, and the organic course of his life was fixed by his own arbitrary choice.

The enemies of the human spirit are many, and the most easily recognized of these is the human will, which creates chaos in the world as it did in the life of Julian Grant."

—Ben Abramson

"It is a book cerebral, emotional and frightful; it is lovely and hideous; it is not an easy book, not one to be picked up casually—nor, I think, one for a lonely house and a windy night and no company save one's own. There is not one single conventional thrill in it; but something is at one's shoulder as one reads."

—Marguerite Steen, *Everyman*

"He has the originality and importance of Emily Brontë and D.H. Lawrence, because in his own way he has, like them, made a clean break with the 'novel of manners' which has always been the weakness of English fiction.

If this novel does not prove to be one of the most discussed books of 1933, something is rotten in the state of fiction."

—Editor, *Everyman*

"...It is a book that stands in a different class from the great bulk of current fiction, not only by virtue of its aim, the scope of its conception, but also for its real depth of thought, its memorable phrases crystalizing long-pondered experience, in addition to its color, humor, satire and deft handing of most baffling situations. This needs to be said at once in any discussion of *Julian Grant.* In criticizing it one is criticizing an absolute achievement. If in some respects it seems to fall short of its highest possibility, that is not because Mr. Houghton is not abundantly gifted to write ninety per cent of our novelists off the earth, but rather because, like Icarus, he flies too near the sun, dares the sheer impossible."

—Geoffrey West, *Bookman*

Kingdoms of the Spirit

"As a young man, pondering on the root-identity of all religions, he had written, swiftly and half miraculously, night after night in a damp Chelsea basement, a series of essays called *Kingdoms of the Spirit*. Each individual life, he argued, is one link in an eternal sequence operating outside time, outside religious tenets, outside mortality. Escaping from the 'Kingdom of Self' man can attain a spiritual reality. The culmination of that progress is the 'Kingdom of Love.'

This 'act of worship' unlocked Houghton for his true vocation. He switched suddenly to novel-writing, but the idea, the inspiration, never left him. Under diverse ingenious plots and narratives, it is still to be found sometimes in an inverted sequence where instead of regeneration the self goes steadily downward, into its personal purgatory or hell. At the end of this soul's journey is 'the Nightmare Life-in-Death' who diced and won the Ancient Mariner. From that doom, after existing with 'a thousand thousand slimy things,' it may be possible to escape.

The way Houghton matched his mysticism with an all-out realistic scene must remain a marvel..."

—Sylvia Norman, *Times Literary Supplement*

Strangers

"This novel is not just the familiar story of husband, wife, and mistress. It is that, and its treatment is such that suspense becomes cumulative with the turning of every page, but it is more than that. Here is the truth about many a marriage. And every character in this book is a world.

You do not watch these worlds, you enter them. Above all, you enter Grantham's secret interior world. You become this man. You understand his strange love for his wife, his imaginative love for his children, his passionate love for his mistress. His conflicts, his remorse, his joys, his sudden ecstasies, his loneliness becomes yours. You wait on tip-toe, as he does, for the coming of the inevitable hour in which the two women will meet. But you do not—and cannot—foresee the circumstances of that meeting.

And it is because you become Grantham and know, therefore, those aspects of his complex nature of which wife and mistress know nothing that you realize why the book is called *Strangers*. Each looks out on a different world. Each seeks a different kind of happiness. Each makes a different demand from destiny.

From the first page there is the almost uncanny sensation that you are entering the world of each character in turn. You become involved in a drama—a drama which penetrates to the depths of your own emotional life."

—Collins Publishers

"This is a very good book....Here, if you like, is ecstasy: the ecstasy of a young girl seeing lovely things day after day with the man she loves. Rarely, so far as I know, has this common experience been transcribed with so much truth and beauty."

—Howard Strong

"Behind Mr. Houghton's novel stands a whole world of individual and striking ideas."

—*Times Literary Supplement*

"*Strangers* is a book which had had such a powerful effect on both my mind and emotions that I find it intensely difficult to write about it. Why? Because it is written with a spiritual intensity that has heightened the author's powers: his observation, his imagination, his sense of form, and his faculty for self-expression....It will cause this book to be read and widely discussed."

—Richard Church

This was Ivor Trent

"Mr. Houghton is a romantic. He is original. He attempts what has been seldom done in modern literature, he tackles spiritual problems in imaginative terms and in consequence has come dangerously near telling the truth about life.

This was Ivor Trent is the story of a man of keener perceptions than most humans, a four-dimensional man prophetic of a future race. We know him through the men he has befriended, the women he has loved, as their images of him are captured and pieced together by a fascinated and curious stranger. An original, amazing and compelling book, a logical growth from *I am Jonathan Scrivener*, and *Julian Grant Loses His Way*."

—Doubleday Doran

"In the opening pages, we see Ivor Trent, an eminent and well-known figure, leave his familiar surroundings and go to a secret life of his own—the existence of which is wholly unknown to his friends. As the result of sudden illness, this mysterious 'underground' life is discovered. His friends are dramatically confronted by the baffling duality of Trent's nature. And—to two women—the discovery is a menacing one.

A unique atmosphere dominates this book. It rivets the attention, and intrigues the imagination. It has suspense and mystery. It is full of dramatic scenes, poignant revelations, intimate relationships. Only Houghton could have written it, and only this age could have inspired it."

—William Heinemann Ltd.

"Mental excitement runs through *This was Ivor Trent*. It is not the same as the excitement aroused by incident, of which there is also no lack, but it is more thrilling and there is probably no one writing fiction today who can communicate it so well as Mr. Houghton can."

—*The Scotsman*

"Claude Houghton is leading the field in mental and intellectual stimulation with *This was Ivor Trent.* I found it as thrilling and tantalizing as any crime story."

—*Daily Mail*

[Letter from Ben Abramson to Claude Houghton]

Our Time of Ripeness: On Writers and the Writers Life, An Afterword

December 7, 1938

Dear Claude,

I am glad the new novel [*Hudson Rejoins the Herd*] is going well, that you are "in" it. Writing is a lonely, cold business, which cannot warm one as do those intangible qualities we derive from friendship and love of humans; it has in it no sympathy and understanding, no tenderness, no murmured word of endearment, no slightest caressing touch. The writer must know more loneliness than most men, for to the loneliness we all know he must add another—he must withdraw himself from living men, and go to dwell in a land peopled with real and living and created beings, but bloodless and without flesh, and though they are real and living they cannot cry to him alone, their spirits cannot touch only his spirit, nor their love console him entirely; they cannot answer his need alone, but must respond to that of all men.

And yet for a time the writer is God. He is fashioning living people, he must shape their destinies, and form their pattern convincingly, so that the people in his book, no matter how fantastic, how bizarre, how extraordinary, shall have in them kinship with all. Was it Thackeray who wept whenever one of his characters died, because to him it was a personal, irremediable loss? It is in this creation, this godship, that the writer knows recompense and solace for loneliness—friends speak to him and he stares at them unseeingly, because for a time he dwells in a far world, and knows the excitement that comes from creation, the ecstatic living warm loneliness that none can share with him.

I am glad your new book is different from *Strangers*, which I am going to read before I write you again. I am glad, very glad, that *Strangers* had a wide sale, and that through contact with it your audience was increased because people who read that book wanted your other books. I am in deepest sympathy not only with the fact that writers need money on which to live—and so often, and so unfairly, need it desperately—but that it is a sweet, unutterably sweet return for labor.

And yet, as I have written you so many times, you are for the few, and you should be glad that you are. When you say that the world's best sellers are the world's best books, you have spoken truth, because they are. But the mob has nothing to do with the long-selling best book. Shakespeare and Marlowe and Keats and Houghton are enduring, they are long-selling, for the very reason that they are for the few. The mob will not read nor buy your books now; the mob will not read or buy your books one hundred years from now; but the few read your books now, and they will read them one hundred years from now. That is why the great artist should be always true to himself and faithful to his individual ability. From year to year, from generation to generation from century to century, it is only the few who keep alive the great books and painting and music.

Thomas Hardy shone with fierce and steady light for fifty long years. He shall endure. Steinbeck has flashed brilliantly for five. Steinbeck's books have a wide sale—he has caught on. But who can tell whether he is the caprice of the generation that has produced radio and cocktails and Hitler—or if in his books are things that shall outlast the mob and be retained by the few? Always, I try to help as much as I possibly can, the Steinbecks and the Houghtons and the Spencers, when in their beginnings their work is not as widely known as my faith in them feels it should be. But whether they become "best sellers" for the mob I do not care—perhaps I even distrust their achieving that. That they should be unknown and unread by the few who matter is wrong and unjust and fantastic; but that writers whom I believe will, and ought to, endure beyond their generation, should achieve the notoriety, and amazing and incredible sale of a popular-with-the-mob "best seller" does not interest me—except that I am happy that they are rewarded financially as they can never be rewarded by the few. All of which does not prevent me from hoping with all my heart that your new book will sell more copies than all your other books combined. I want and hope and pray that the sale of your books will climb and climb and climb. I shall always do everything I can to further that, because I have boundless faith in what you do, and because I know also that money is important to you, as it is to me and everyone else. But I am afraid, dear Claude, that I do not want you to leap to a dizzying height which would mean nothing.

When the new book nears completion, I will make a special effort to sell a manuscript, since that would be the most opportune time. I will write you further about this when I have had a chance to give it more thought.

If it means your coming to the States, then by all the gods! I will do everything in my power to sell one for I am anxious to see you, and I trust that I shall see you. Not only should you come west to Chicago but you should go farther west and farther, to where the real prairies swell against the sky, to where the desert with its far distances, its impregnable harsh beauty, its awful and overwhelming reaches of silence can touch you and wipe you clean and make you realize as you have never realized before that we are small, small; and still beyond, into the Northwest, with its green valleys, and long-descending waterfalls, and its mighty, towering trees. I hope to be in New York sometime this spring. I suppose your visit will come late in the year?

That you should have a breathing space after twelve long years of writing is more important than my eager desire to see you. You say that an account of my activities sends you into the fourth dimension. All that you have accomplished in the last twelve years in hard, solid, finished tasks, pleases you, not in the fourth dimension, but somewhere even beyond Einstein's ken. Slowly the *Miscellany* is assembling and rousing from its long sleep. I could not possibly think of a better subject than *The Individual Writer*, especially from the angles of—what is he, does he matter, will he survive? You say you could work in something about book collectors—how you would do that I do not know; my instant thought is that it is the individual writers who survive, as I have written so lengthily above—it is the individual writers who are collected by subsequent generations—the Wildes, the Shaws, the Joyces, the Houghtons, the Dickens. If you could get your article to me by February 1, I would be grateful.

Do not grieve too much that the world has a surfeit of megalomania, of torture and oppression, and of chaos. For Shakespeare said, "Men must endure their going hence, even as their coming hither; ripeness is all." There is always chaos, and we must endure, as man has always endured. The world is old, but man is young. We are not yet out of the jungle. There is a relation between your life and mine and the centuries of time, for each man contains within him all that has befallen every man. Our defect is a too great nearness to ourselves. With perspective, we see our own vices without heat reflected distantly in Solomon, Alcibiades, and Cataline. "Ripeness is all." That, dear Claude, makes chaos endurable. We cannot savour the best of life until we are ripe to understand and to desire them, to hold them dear, and realize that all the illusionary things we saw beyond them in our youth, are but illusions.

This is our time of ripeness, and who shall not say that it makes chaos not only endurable, but desirable, since amid chaos we can gather to ourselves and hold close the friends, the music, the Hardys, the Steinbecks, the Houghtons—the pig's knuckle and the kraut—the gin and bitters—the memories of fair women and those not so fair, that heaven of a madding world.

Sincerely yours,

Ben

Claude Houghton: A Brief Bibliography

Twelve Lyrics
Margate [c. 1912].

The Phantom Host and Other Verse
London: Elkin Mathews, 1917.

The Tavern of Dreams, A Volume of Verse
London: Grant Richards, Ltd., 1919.

Judas, A Tragedy in Three Acts
London: C.W. Daniel, Ltd., 1922.
Boston: The Four Seas Company, 1927.

In the House of the High Priest: A Drama in One Act
London: C.W. Daniel Co, 1923.
Boston: The Four Seas Company, 1927.

The Kingdoms of the Spirit
London: The C.W. Daniel Company, 1924.
London: The C.W. Daniel Company, 1938.
London: The C.W. Daniel Company, 1947.

Neighbors
London: Robert Holden & Co., Ltd., 1926.
New York: Henry Holt & Co., [abridged edition] 1927.
Chicago: Argus Book Shop, [First complete American Edition], 1937.

London: Collins, 1938.

Some Rise by Sin

Woking, England: Privately printed by Unwin Brothers at the Gresham Press, 1926.

London: Hutchinson, 1956.

The Riddle of Helena

London: Robert Holden & Co., Ltd., 1927.

Prague: Symposion, (Trade Edition) 1933.

(as above in a Limited Edition of 30)

(as above in a Limited Edition of 300)

London: Collins (New Edition), 1934.

Chicago: Argus Bookshop, 1934.

Crisis

London: Thornton Butterworth, Ltd., 1929.

London: Thornton Butterworth, Ltd., 1932.

London: Thornton Butterworth, Ltd., 1936.

New York: Harper & Brothers, 1929.

The Last Command (a novelization of the play of the same name by Lajos Biro, illustrated with scenes from the movie, a Paramount production starring Emil Jannings. London: Readers Library Publishing Co., 1929.

The Sins of the Fathers (a novelization based on the film of the same name, illustrated with scenes from the movie, a Paramont production starring Emil Jannings). London: The Readers Library Publishing Co., 1930.

The Captain of the Guard (Based on *La Marseillaise*, by Houston Branch). London: Readers Library Publishing Co., 1930.

I am Jonathan Scrivener

London: Thornton Butterworth, Ltd., 1930.
New York: Simon and Schuster, 1930.
London: Thornton Butterworth, Ltd., 1933.
Garden City, NY: Doubleday Doran & Company, 1934.
Garden City, NY: Doubleday Doran & Company, 1935.
London: Eyre & Spottiswoode, 1942.
London: Eyre & Spottiswoode, 1946.
London: Collins, 1950.
Published as *Je Suis Jonathan Scrivener*, traduit de l'anglais par Jean Rosenthal. Preface by Henry Miller. Paris: Corrêa, 1954.
Bath [England]: Chivers, 1977.

A Hair Divides

London: Thornton Butterworth, Ltd., 1930.
Garden City, New York: Doubleday Doran & Co., Inc., 1931.
Stockholm: Wahlström and Widstrand, published as *Sin Egen Fange*, 1931.
Paris: ?, 1938. Published as *L'epaisser d'un cheveu*, traduit de l'anglais par Louis Postif, Illustrations de J. Simont.

The Big Trail (novelized by Claude Houghton). London: The Readers Library Publishing Co., Ltd., 1931. A Fox Movie Tone production directed by Raoul Walsh, starring John Wayne and Marguerite Churchill. Bound with John Wilson's *The Man Who Came Back.*

Chaos is Come Again

London: Thornton Butterworth, Ltd., 1932

Garden City, New York: Doubleday Doran & Co., 1932.

Stockholm: Wahlström and Widstrand, published as *Den Originella Familjen*, 1933.

London: Thornton Butterworth, Ltd., 1934.

Julian Grant Loses His Way

Garden City, New York: Doubleday Doran & Co., 1933.

Stockholm: Wahlström and Widstrand, 1933.

London: William Heinemann, Ltd., 1934.

Three Fantastic Tales (Limited Edition) with a frontispiece by John Farleigh and a preface by Clemence Dane. London: Frederick C. Joiner, 1934.

This was Ivor Trent

London:William Heinemann, 1935.

Garden City, NY: Doubleday Doran & Co., 1935.

The Passing of the Third Floor Back

London: Queensway Press, 1935.

Christina

London: William Heinemann, Ltd., 1936.
Garden City, NY: Doubleday Doran & Co., 1936.
London: Collins, 1950.

The Beast

Illustrated by Alfred E. Kerr. Limited Edition.
Belfast: Quota Press, 1936.
Belfast: Quota Press, 1937.

Strangers

London: Collins, 1937.
New York: Macmillan Co., 1938.

Hudson Rejoins the Herd

London: Collins, 1939.
New York: Macmillan Co., 1939.
London: Albatross, 1947.

All Change, Humanity!

London: Collins, 1942.

Six Lives and a Book

London: Collins, 1943.

Passport to Paradise

London: Collins, 1944.

Transformation Scene

London: Collins, 1946.

The Quarrel
London: Collins, 1948.

Birthmark
London: Collins, 1950.

The Enigma of Conrad Stone
London: Collins, 1952.

At the End of the Road
London: Hutchinson, 1953.

The Clock Ticks
London: Hutchinson, 1954.

More Lives Than One
London: Hutchinson, 1957.

Index

Irving Stettner

On Henry Miller and the Wo Hop Mystery

along with the facsimile of a business card containing a brief note from Henry Miller

Poet, artist and longtime friend of Henry Miller, Irving Stettner went off like a Chinese firecracker when he received a business card from the Wo Hop restaurant that included a message on back written in Miller's hand during 1979. Irving tells us the story behind the Wo Hop card but he doesn't stop there:

> *"I've always dreamed of one day writing about Henry Miller," he said, "but extensively—a book, nothing less. However, while we're on the subject..."*

And with this Stettner takes a deep breath and extends his essay to include a look at Henry Miller, the man and the writer. He speaks of Miller's influence, the "message" of his work and what the uninitiated can expect in reading Miller's prose for the first time.

On Henry Miller and the Wo Hop Mystery

8 1/5 x 5 1/5 inches; 32 pages; Stapled spine; Printed in an edition of 250 copies; ISBN: 0-9634136-2-2; $12.00.

Note: Each copy issued with a facsimile of the Wo Hop business card that has Miller's text reproduced on back. This booklet now available from the publisher:

Roger Jackson, *Publisher*
339 Brookside Drive
Ann Arbor, Michigan 48105

Henry Miller

Farewell from France:
A Letter to Huntington Cairns
April 30, 1939

Dear Huntington,

This is one of those gloomy Sundays in Europe when the impending catastrophe seems more than ever certain, one in which my own fate seems bound up with the fate of Europe. I am taking the occasion to give you a few further facts about myself, which will be of interest to the biographers later, in the event that I am separated from my belongings—notebooks, unpublished manuscripts, etc., or wiped out by an unexpected air raid, because this time, if the Germans strike, I am positive they will strike before declaring war.

Sitting at the Place Paul Verlaine this morning I was reflecting on how much I have written since September, 1924, when I definitely embarked on the career of a writer. I had begun a bit before that, but I was not sure of myself until that day in September, 1924, when I threw up my job without a moment's notice, and decided never to work again but to do nothing but write.

Briefly, and as best I remember, here is the record. I began writing in my father's tailor shop a 5 West 31st St., N.Y., opposite the Wolcott Hotel, after teaching myself how to type. That was about 1912, when I was twenty-one. I wrote long literary and humorous letters to my friends, which were really disguised essays on everything. Wrote out of boredom, because I was not interested in my father's business. During this period the first thing I remember writing, as a piece of writing in itself, was a long essay on Nietzsche's *Anti-Christ*. I must preface this by saying that I had gone to work at the age of 18, having left City College, N.Y., in the first few months. At this period...

Publisher's Note

Huntington Cairns was a lawyer from Baltimore, Maryland, who worked for the U.S. Treasury Department. His position was that of Special Advisor, whose responsibility was in determining which books were "obscene" (and therefore would be intercepted by customs officials) and which books were of a sexual content that could be considered "works of art" and thus allowed entry into the United States.

The letter reprinted here, part of a correspondence that would run through 1959, was written the month before Miller's departure from Paris; it signaled the end of a 9-year residence during which his most famous books were written. It is a personal statement about his life and a self-evaluation about his success as a writer.

Trade Edition
(ISBN: 0-9634136-5-3)

36-page booklet in wrappers; 4 1/4 inches x 5 1/2 inches; Printed on Peppercorn Bond; 1 copy = $5; 3 copies = $10; 10+ copies = $2.00 each.

Limited Edition
(ISBN: 0-9634136-7-2)

100 copies have been printed on Speckletone® Old Green text, individually handbound in boards and covered with decorative paper. The Limited Edition is signed and numbered by the publisher. This edition only contains a reproduction of "Henry Miller: The Dapper" an original frontispiece sketch by Ben Davies that has been stamped in gold foil. Note: The Limited Edition has a trim size of 5 1/2 x 8 1/2 inches, larger than the Trade Edition. $60

Roger Jackson, *Publisher*
339 Brookside Drive
Ann Arbor, Michigan 48105

Henry Miller

The Mezzotints

In 1925, 36 years before Henry Miller received instant fame at the American publication of his *Tropic of Cancer*, (a book banned in this country for decades due to its sexual content), he wrote and published a series of literary sketches which he called his *Mezzotints*. They had the appearance of a small handbill, were printed on color paper and measured 6 x 9 inches. Both Miller and his wife June sold them door-to-door, as well as in the speakeasies and restaurants of Greenwich Village. The titles of these sketches are:

Dawn Travellers — *A Bowery Phoenix*
Make Beer for Man — *The Awakening*
Christianity at the Sink — *Dance Hall*
If You're Dying, Choose a Mausoleum — *Circe*

This publication consists of:

A facsimile edition of 8 individual handbills which Miller called his *Mezzotints*. Size, color of paper used and type style has all been selected to correspond with the originals.

A 40-page booklet which includes a detailed history of the *Mezzotints*. Wrapper is made from Classic Laid® Peppered Bronze paper.

Issued in a domestically produced, handmade presen-tation folder covered with maroon binders cloth and raspberry Italia paper, an acid free, mould paper of 100% cotton imported from Italy.

Published in an edition of 400 copies; 6 x 9 inches;
ISBN = 0-9634136-2-7; $40.

Roger Jackson, *Publisher*
339 Brookside Drive
Ann Arbor, Michigan 48105

Elmer Gertz

A Fabulous Miller Deposition That Did Not Take Place

In 1961, while a 27 year ban on importation of Miller's *Tropic of Cancer* was still in effect, Grove Press courageously published this book in the United States. In its wake, more than 60 lawsuits were filed in order to restrict its sale and distribution. Elmer Gertz, famed attorney and specialists in First Amendment rights, was retained by Grove Press to defend the charges against *Tropic of Cancer* in the Chicago area. Henry Miller, then 69 years old, could have been summoned by opposing counsel to answer the following questions:

"Would you let your children read this book? "What redeeming values does your book have? "Do you know the legal definition of obscenity?" "What did you try to accomplish in your now notorious book?" "Can't sex be described without a continuous flow of dirty words?" "Do you think your book is acceptable in any civilized American community?"

Friend and attorney during the last 17 years of Miller's life, Elmer Gertz has provided both the questions and answers to this imaginary deposition and provides the necessary historical context to further the readers understanding. This unique scenario gives us the words and manner in which Henry Miller would most likely have answered the accusations brought against him and the book that caused him so much trouble.

4 x 9 1/2 inches; 16 pages; Stapled spine; Printed in an edition of 500 copies; ISBN: 0-9634136-5-5; $5.00. Signed Limited Edition of 100 copies is also avaliable at $15.00. ISBN: 0-9634136-6-2.

Roger Jackson, *Publisher*
339 Brookside Drive
Ann Arbor, Michigan 48105

Roger Jackson/William E. Ashley

Henry Miller: A Personal Archive

At the time of Henry Miller's death, in June 1980 at the age of 88, his manuscripts, letters and ephemera were put in storage. This material has now been catalogue and is being offered for sale. This collection includes letters from Lawrence Durrell, Anaïs Nin and Alfred Perlès, sketches drawn in notebooks, wall charts, drafts, manuscripts and business records. The text of unpublished manuscripts and letters are reproduced in over 60 illustrations. Included are descriptions of unpublished books and plays, letters from admirers, checks, tax records, signed contracts and over 1,000 photographs. This catalogue is completely indexed.

100 copies of *Henry Miller: A Personal Archive* have been specially bound in boards and covered with illustrated blue paper. This edition has matching blue endpapers with a slit in the back paste-down that contains an authentic advertising insert from 1968 that was written, published and distributed by Miller to promote his book *To Paint is to Love Again, Including Semblance of a Devoted Past*. This 4 x 6 inch insert is included with each copy sold. This edition has been signed and numbered by Miller's children. Catalogue compiled by Roger Jackson and William E. Ashley.

Henry Miller: A Personal Archive

5 1/2 x 8 1/2 inches; 316 pages; Casebound; Illustrated; Limited Edition of 100 singed and numbered copies; ISBN: 0-9634136-9-4; $75.

Roger Jackson, *Publisher*
339 Brookside Drive
Ann Arbor, Michigan 48105

Henry Miller/John Bagnole

A Certain Kind of Madness!!
Henry Miller and The Bibliography of Primary Sources

This is the first separate publication of Henry Miller's *Preface* to the recently published descriptive bibliography, *Henry Miller: A Bibliography of Primary Sources*. Written in 1978 approximately 2 years before his death, it had remained unpublished until 1993. The master writer takes a glance at—what was then in typescript form—hundreds of pages detailing his literary output spanning more than half a century. The *Preface* is about his work, but as always with Miller, it's also a look at the man himself, his biases, his beliefs.

One must be possessed of a certain kind of madness, I feel, to compile a bibliography...To collect all the material amassed in this huge tome represents the labor of a prisoner tunneling his way out of a jail over a period of months and years. One can only imagine what cunning and ingenuity it required to gather all this information.. —H.M.

In its first publication anywhere, John W. Bagnole's essay *The Colossus of Brooklyn*, takes an enchanting yet critical look at the *Bibliography* from the standpoint of a reader, collector and scholar. His style, a unique blending of essay and review, notes the importance of this bibliographical study of one of America's most prolific and most misunderstood writers.

A Certain Kind of Madness!!

8 1/2 x 5 1/2 inches; 32 pages; Stapled spine; Printed in an edition of 250 copies; ISBN: 0-9634136-4-3; $7.50.

Roger Jackson, *Publisher*
339 Brookside Drive
Ann Arbor, Michigan 48105

Henry Miller:
A Bibliography of Primary Sources
Volumes I & II
1,686 pages • 490 items illustrated
A CERTAIN KIND OF
MADNESS!!
Henry Miller
Land
der Erinnerung
Sammlung Luchterhand
THEATRE MAUBEL - MICHEL GALABRU
COMPAGNIE
PICPUS
TROPIQUE
DU
CANCER
HENRY
MILLER
The Air-Conditioned
Nightmare
Henry Miller
Panther
IT'S A BIRD
IT'S A PLANE
IT'S SUPERMAN
Henry Miller
Tropique du Cancer
roman
Denoël
Henry Miller's
murder the
murderer
HENRY MILLER
GREECE

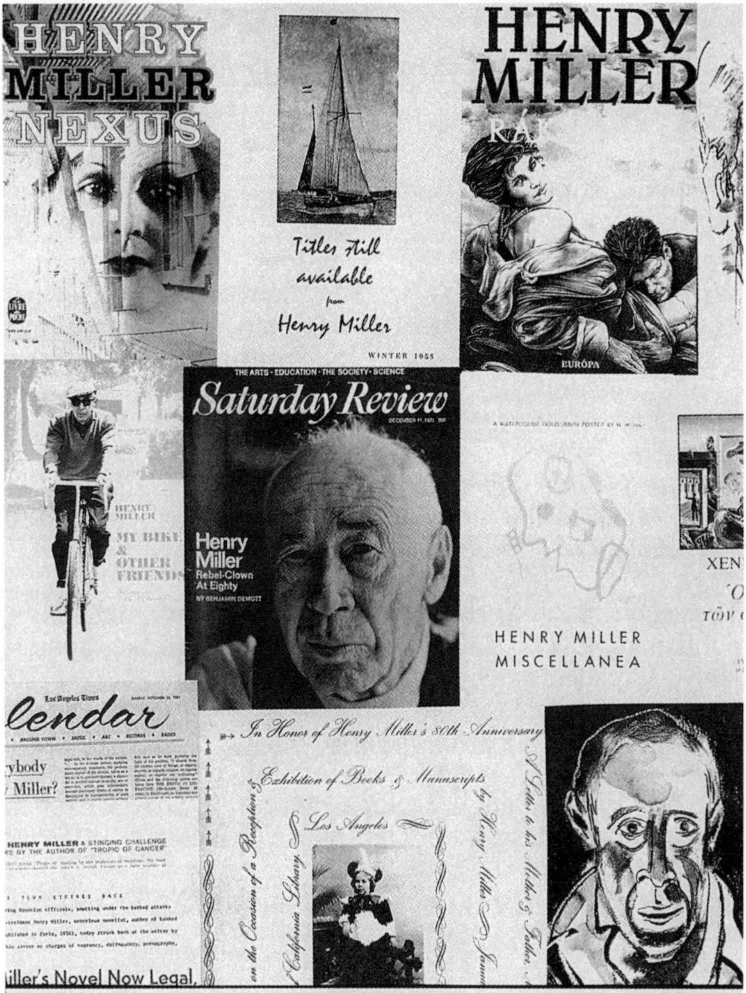

Volume I
Roger Jackson / Larry Shifreen
ISBN: 0-9634135-0-0
1,160 pages
365 items illustrated
53-page Index
$95

Volume II
Roger Jackson / Wm. E. Ashley
ISBN 0-9634136-6-X
526 pages
125 items illustrated
44-page Index
$45

Purchase Orders Welcomed • Satisfaction Guaranteed
Copies of both Volumes available from either:

Roger Jackson
339 Brookside Dr.
Ann Arbor, MI 48105
(313) 665-4614

Wm E. Ashley
PO Box 1122
Pismo Beach, CA 93448
(805) 773-2823
(phone or fax)

Craig Peter Standish

Henry Miller: A Book of Tributes, 1931-1994

125 Individual Contributions including essays from:

Norman Mailer, Anaïs Nin, Erica Jong, Lawrence Durrell, William Carlos Williams, John Lennon, John Cowper Powys, Alfred Perlès, Karl Shapiro along with more than 100 others have their say in the form of poetry, essays, tributes, memoirs, art work and photographs produced over the last 63 years on the subject of Henry Miller. *More than half of the material has never before been published in any form, and was in fact written exclusively for inclusion in this book.* Much of the material that was previously published has been out of print for almost half a century.

These contributions come from Miller's friends, neighbors, publishers, lovers, translators, biographers, bibliographers, lawyers, readers and collectors.

This volume also contains:

The first English language appearance of *A Transfertrotted Foxenbite*, a burlesque fairy tale by Henry Miller

Anaïs Nin's previously unpublished notes of Miller's *Tropic of Cancer*

5 1/2 x 8 1/2 inches; 720 pages; Casebound; Illustrated with dozens of previously unpublished photographs and reproductions of his art work; ISBN 0-941415-0-7; $45. Published by Craig Peter Standish. Available from:

Future Titles

Questions About Henry Miller That No One Ever Asked Me—with answers
—Bern Porter

Questions About Henry Miller That No One Ever Asked Me—with answers
—Mary V. Dearborn

"I've got the cosmic blues..."
—Henry Miller

Visits with Henry Miller: A Woman's Point of View
—Mamie Gertz

for ARGUS BOOKS, INC.
—Ben Abramson

Heros for All Time: Little Jimmy's History Lesson
–Roger Jackson

Roger Jackson, *Publisher*
339 Brookside Drive
Ann Arbor, Michigan 48105

Writers Three: A Literary Exchange
was printed in Dexter, Michigan,
during August, 1995.

Printing was limited to 1000 copies,
distributed in the following manner:

A 650-copy American Trade Edition published by Roger Jackson

A 250-copy European Edition published by Karl Orend, Alyscamps Press

A 100-copy American Limited Edition, specially bound with decorative end-papers, numbered and signed by Deborah Benson. This edition only contains a limited edition reproduction of *Meeting Henry Miller*, an essay written by Deborah Benson.

This is copy No.